THE RUPTURE OF SERENITY

D1564289

THE RUPTURE
OF SERENITY
External Intrusions and
Psychoanalytic Technique

Aisha Abbasi

KARNAC

First published in 2014 by
Karnac Books Ltd
118 Finchley Road
London NW3 5HT

British Library Cataloguing in Publication Data

A C.I.P. for this book is available from the British Library

ISBN-13: 978-1-78049-195-0

Typeset by V Publishing Solutions Pvt Ltd., Chennai, India

Printed in Great Britain

www.karnacbooks.com

*For Aamer
with all my love, always,
and
for Azad, Sofia, and Rania,
who make it all worthwhile*

CONTENTS

PART III: WHEN MACHINES INTRUDE UPON
CLINICAL SPACE

PART IV: WHEN POLITICAL EVENTS INTRUDE UPON
CLINICAL SPACE

ACKNOWLEDGEMENTS

To Salman Akhtar, my dear friend and mentor, for helping me, with your kind and thoughtful listening, to gather my scattered ideas and bring them together. This book would not have come into existence without such help, and for this, and much more, I thank you.

To my husband Aamer, for cheering me on as I wrote this book; for sternly reminding me of the deleterious effects on my health of not getting enough sleep; for tolerating my early-morning alarms and late nights; for helping in the kitchen and with school activities and swim lessons; for occasionally yelling, "When is this thing going to get *done*?"; and most of all, for loving me through it all and keeping it *real*, I thank you.

To my son Azad and my daughter-in-law Sofia for cheerfully negotiating the mix of my desire to write this book during the same year we were planning your wedding; for being the wonderful young adults you are; for your encouragement, love, and support in everything I take on; and most of all, for choosing each other to be with, so that we have two terrific people to love instead of just one, I thank you.

To my daughter Rania, for understanding that even though I adore you, we needed to forgo some of our precious time together while

I wrote this book; for the bouts of "giggleitis" you spark in me; for the excellent stories about your world of school, friends, music, and celebrities; for still wanting me to go shopping with you; and for being the funny, sassy kid you are, I thank you (and yes, we are going to play mini-golf *now*!).

To my mother, Dr Razia Hussain, and my mother-in-law, Mrs Rukia Abbasi, for helping shape me and my children in ways that allow us to navigate the world better; and for being a terrific support for all of us, in many different ways, I thank you.

In memory of my father, Colonel Ghulam Hussain, and my father-in-law, Mr Khaled Abbasi, for being the strong, sometimes stubborn (but secretly soft-hearted), sweet, feisty men you were; and for your enduring gifts of love and courage, I thank you.

To my analyst, Dale Boesky, for helping me figure out what happened in my life, mourn what was sad, and celebrate what was—and is—wonderful; for understanding not only what others might have done to me, but also, clearly, what I do to others; for letting me take the time, with you, I needed to; for being unafraid to fight with me and for me; and for helping me see that contrary to my childhood ideas, I actually have very little control over what happens in my life—so I might as well just go with the flow and enjoy it—I thank you.

To my siblings, my husband's siblings, and our nieces and nephews, for being the loving, smart, accomplished people you are; for letting me lean on you, intellectually and emotionally; for being fun to compete with (my siblings) and a pleasure to see you come into your own (for our young ones); and for always, always standing strong with me and my family, I thank you.

To Mayer Subrin, for sharing with me your particular and beautiful way of listening to patients; for listening endlessly to me over egg-white omelettes at The Gallery; for always rooting for me; for introducing me to the Group for the Study of the Psychoanalytic Process (GSPP); and for your gift of sturdy friendship, I thank you.

To Lena Ehrlich, for being not only a loving and deeply trusted friend, but also a critic par excellence of my analytic thinking and writing; for being there for me, day after day, even across thousands of miles as we each travelled to our respective motherlands; for all this and much I do not have space to describe, I thank you.

To my dear friends Krishna Gupta, Ellie Kulis, Laura Leacock, Kim Leary, Julie Nagel, Jia Naqvi, Sally Rosenberg, Anu Sarkar, Nigar Yousuf, and Shirin Zaman, for your unswerving love and encouragement in the writing of this book and in the rest of my life; for staying in touch via texts, phone calls, and emails; for discussions over dinner, coffee, and brunches; for sharing my laughter and wiping away my tears, I thank you.

To all my friends and colleagues at GSPP, for taking me on when I was a rookie; for helping me become an analyst with a broad view of the human experience, thanks to the wisdom and the depth and breadth of analytic knowledge I am exposed to when I sit in meetings with you twice a year; and for unstinting love and support in matters both personal and professional, I thank you.

To my patients, for helping me plumb greater depths within myself by letting me know you more intimately; for teaching me wisdom and humility and a greater respect for human suffering every time I work with you; for trusting me with your feelings; and for allowing me to be your analyst, I thank you.

To my editor, Barbara Nordin, for your sustained commitment to helping me write this, my first book of analytic stories; for your incisive editorial help; and for your firm but cheerful attitude when I had thoughts of extending the deadline, I thank you.

And finally, to my publisher at Karnac, Oliver Rathbone, for giving me a chance to put this collection in print; for your thoughtful, wise, and succinct comments during the preparation of this manuscript; and for letting me think through and implement changes along the way, I thank you.

ABOUT THE AUTHOR

Aisha Abbasi, MD, graduated from Fatima Jinnah Medical College in Lahore, Pakistan. She moved to America with her husband, Aamer, in 1987 and completed a residency in psychiatry at the Henry Ford Hospital, Detroit, MI. She trained to become a psychoanalyst at the Michigan Psychoanalytic Institute, where she is now a training and supervising analyst. She has presented and published on a variety of analytic topics, and is currently co-chair of a discussion group, "The birth of an analysis in the mind of the analyst: From evaluation, to recommendation, and beyond", which convenes annually at the winter meeting of the American Psychoanalytic Association. Her collection of Urdu poetry, *Ek Dunya Meray Andar Hai* (*The World Within*), was published in Pakistan in 2007 and in the U.S. in 2009. She lives in West Bloomfield, Michigan, with her husband and daughter and the family's cocker spaniel, Raja Riley. Her son and daughter-in-law live close by, ensuring good times at the nearby family cottage during the beautiful Michigan summers and lively adventures together, all year round.

INTRODUCTION

This book was written as a life is lived: in bits and pieces, over time, its chaotic colours spilling onto the pages—not neatly and in an orderly fashion, but rather in an exhilarating cascade of feelings, memories, and experiences. I wish I could say that I thought it all out carefully and regularly, sat down every day or three days a week to write: I didn't. I felt that this book had to be written not as *the* book but rather as *a* book, so that I could share certain experiences, dilemmas, and accounts of analytic treatments that had challenged me, in intriguing ways, to hone my analytic skills. This is, essentially, a collection of analytic stories, and my hope is that I have been able to write clearly—and with as little jargon as possible—so that it can be understood and enjoyed not only by an analytic audience, but also by a layperson. I believe that this is the best way we can convey what we do to those who are not familiar with the work of psychoanalysts. It is only through such communication that we build necessary bridges with our communities—for I think of psychoanalysis not as some mysterious and sacred scientific cult, but as a way of understanding our minds and our lives that can benefit many, including those not in treatment.

The title of this book contains a core of irony. There is, of course, no such thing as true and complete serenity; this is an unrealistic ideal. In the not-so-distant past, psychoanalysts liked to believe that we function in a kind of therapeutic cocoon, where the analytic dyad analyses while life goes on outside. This is no longer considered to be true. In recent decades, there has been much greater awareness of the impact of the analyst's life situation—and feelings—on the analytic work. Major external events, such as the "September 11th" attacks, have spurred great interest over the last decade in how the world outside can enter analytic sessions. Being an immigrant female analyst, for instance, I was quickly made aware of my patients' reactions (both positive and negative) to the differences between us, and found that they entered the analytic work in intriguing ways. All of this gave rise to a number of papers on this topic that I have either presented at meetings or published. A few others were still in draft form, and still others were just beginning, in my mind, to coalesce. Hence this book.

I am sometimes asked which psychoanalytic theory I follow. Although originally trained in the modern conflict/contemporary structural theory, I now agree with Scarfone (2011):

> I believe that no theory can ever be expected to give an exhaustive explanation of a case [...] a case that can be explained away teaches us nothing. [...] I rather hold that if the theory is of any use, then it should serve the case not so much by explaining as by opening new paths before us. Paths that might have gone unnoticed without the theory, but also paths which may pose new problems to that same theory. In other words, the theory should be as much alive and open to transformation as the case material with which it deals. (p. 92)

I have organised this book into four parts, each of which addresses a different kind of external intrusion. The topics are self-explanatory, and I will leave the reader to discover the details. Finally, I want to borrow a story from one of Eissler's classic papers:

> I recall a young woman who, in her fifth month of pregnancy, came to August Aichhorn's Child Guidance Clinic, requesting advice about the rearing of the baby she was expecting. She had heard so much, she continued, about the bad effect a mother may have on the growing child and wished to avert the necessity of later self-reproaches. Aichhorn replied, after a moment of reflection, that she

should have her baby and return to the clinic a half year later and report on how she had raised it. Then he would show her the mistakes she had made. (1958, p. 229)

This book of mine has been about nine months in the making, from start to finish. It is time to let it go, so that its merits and mistakes can be assessed by those most qualified to do so. my readers.

Aisha Abbasi, MD

PART I

WHEN EVENTS IN THE ANALYST'S LIFE INTRUDE UPON CLINICAL SPACE

CHAPTER ONE

The analyst's infertility and subsequent pregnancy

Introduction

Significant events occur in every analyst's life. Some of these may never directly affect the analyses we are conducting, and thus there will likely be no reason for the analyst to discuss them with patients. Others might enter our analytic work indirectly—as I will discuss in Chapter Three—because a patient has been informed by others about events in the analyst's private life. Still others might be events that directly affect the frame of an analytic treatment, such as the analyst's illness (which could include ongoing treatment); the illness, death, or impending death of a family member; and events that necessitate a major change in the schedule or require a flexible schedule. In the latter case, the analyst must decide how to best deal with "telling" or "not telling" her patients about what has caused, is causing, or will cause a disruption in their regular meetings.

Whether one tells or doesn't tell, the analyst also has to be on the lookout for the meaning of the telling or not telling, as well as patients' reactions to the disruption itself; their feelings, if they have been told, about the events; and their feelings about what they imagine is happening if they have not been. No part of this is easy. Nor are there easy answers to the questions, "*Should* I tell my patients about this?", "*When* should I tell my patients about this?", or "*How much* should I tell my patients about this?" In addition, the answers may be different for each analyst-patient dyad. We are all guided in general by our foundational concepts of theory and technique, but these become interwoven, over time, with our individual personality styles and what comes naturally and feels right for each of us. Each analyst also has to take into account each patient's needs, strengths, and vulnerabilities, given what she knows about the patient's history, while being mindful of where the analysis is at that point.

This chapter describes one such series of events in my life, my struggle to sort out how best to handle this in my work with patients, and the route I ultimately took. Over a long period, I suffered from secondary infertility, which led to a sequence of events: treatment, the treatment's failure, and, ultimately, natural conception. I will present clinical material from one analysis to illustrate a patient's reactions to this series of events at different stages.

Background to clinical material

In early 2000 I was thirty-eight years old, four years past the completion of my formal analytic education, and fully immersed in a vibrant and busy analytic practice. My husband and I had a twelve-year-old child and had been struggling for a number of years to have a second child. I had already gone through two surgeries and the less invasive treatments for the kind of infertility that is caused by severe endometriosis. My doctors and the nursing staff kindly—if not entirely correctly—referred to what I had been going through as "treatments for fertility" rather than treatments for infertility. After much back and forth, my husband and I decided that it was time to move on to in vitro fertilisation (IVF). We discussed the options with our infertility specialist, who said that given the success rate (at that time) of IVF at the centre with which he was connected, I would probably have to go through four IVFs before he would recommend that I not keep trying.

After more research, we consulted with a physician in another state whose success rate for IVF with women in my age group was fifty per cent for each attempt. He recommended that I have only two IVFs, and if that did not work, he would not recommend more attempts—in other words, if it was going to work, it would work with two attempts.

The entire sequence, from initial tests through treatments, would mean about six months of periodically being out of town, compared to a little over a year in town. Given the emotional and physical toll that we knew each IVF cycle can take on a couple—and indeed the whole family—my husband and I decided that the option of fewer IVFs would work better for us, even though it would involve air travel back and forth and more extended periods of time away from work and out of town. Neither option was perfect, but that one felt easier for us emotionally and more expedient.

And what about my patients? My husband's work allowed him significant flexibility in terms of being away, but this was not the case with my analytic practice. My patients knew I had a certain routine with times I took off during the year for vacations, conferences, and holidays, and occasionally I would cancel on short notice for emergencies. With IVF, however, I would not be able to predict when I would need to leave town. Our local treatment centre would work with the out-of-state physician, monitoring me during the first part of each treatment cycle and following the treatment he prescribed. At a certain point in the treatment cycle, however, I would be told that I should go to the out-of-town centre within roughly two days to complete the treatment cycle. I would then have to cancel patients for between ten days to two weeks; to further complicate matters, the exact timeframe could not be predetermined.

Being infertile when one wants a child is a difficult and complex situation. I have written (Abbasi, 2011) about the frustration of infertility and of not being able to do what most people can do naturally and easily, stating that this "often brings about a reactivation of old losses and narcissistic vulnerabilities" (p. 366). Allison and Doria-Medina (1999) have referred to "the invasion that the reproductive act between lovers suffers because of the intervention of a medical team that appears to have omnipotent powers to give or withhold a baby and promotes intense transferential feelings of dependency, infantilisation, and vulnerability" (p. 163). These aspects of infertility are difficult enough on their own—both for the couple and for the individuals. Added to this were my worries about our twelve-year-old's well being during this extended period of time. Further compounding my distress was the concern for my patients and the impact my sudden departures and erratic absences would have on them—along with my altered and, in all likelihood, decreased ability to be optimally analytic and of use to them.

I struggled with what—if anything—to tell my patients, when I should tell them, and how. Abend (1982) writes about the paucity of literature on this topic, commenting on:

> [...] the evident disinclination to study, describe, and report on the problem of the technical management of the analyst's illness. This is especially unfortunate since such observations are needed in order to provide reliable and convincing answers to the questions I have attempted to highlight. Under what circumstances, if any, and for which patients, if any, is it advantageous to provide factual information about the analyst's illness? What are the advantages of doing so? What are the difficulties attendant thereon, and what problems ensue if information is not provided? We do not have definitive answers to these questions as yet. A thorough and honest attempt to illuminate this topic is long overdue, and its investigation will be of benefit to many analysts and their patients. (p. 379)

I read all the literature I could find on the topic of disclosure in similar situations and discussed the matter with several colleagues. Finally, I decided to inform my patients that I was struggling with secondary infertility and was about to begin a series of treatments that would, over the next six months, periodically require me to cancel—on short notice—appointments scheduled for the following ten to fourteen days. I added that these were the most basic facts, and that if they had questions they wanted to ask me, that day or later, I hoped that our work would facilitate their being able to do so: their questions, and how we dealt with them, might reveal dilemmas and complex choices for us to negotiate, such as what would be truly helpful for them to know—and why—and whether boundaries were being crossed or too much reality introduced into the analysis. At the same time, I felt that these dilemmas, how we understood them over time, and how we dealt with them would ultimately deepen our work together.

It would be incorrect to say that I arrived at the above decision for some particularly rational or brilliantly thought-through analytic reason; I simply did what I believed would allow me to be most optimally analytic with my patients. It was also the route that felt the simplest and most straightforward, given the strain I was under, my personality style, and my way of working as an analyst in general. There are times in analytic work when each of us has to figure out our own way of dealing with a particular analytic dilemma, and it might not be possible for us to explain fully why we chose the solution we did. I do remember thinking that in the months to come, I would be in a state of great emotional upheaval, pumped up with high doses of hormones, and undergoing a variety of medical and surgical procedures. The thought of having to suddenly announce to my patients, without any explanation, that I needed to cancel a batch of upcoming sessions (for visits to the local treatment centre), followed by another announcement that in a couple of days I would be leaving for two weeks—*and* repeating this abrupt routine twice over a four to six month period—seemed grotesque to me and unfair to my patients. I realised only much later that had I not decided to explain my reasons, I might not have been able to deal with my patients' fantasies about the sudden departures—or, in my vulnerable state, their feelings of hurt and rage about being so abruptly and repeatedly abandoned by me.

So even as I thought that my telling my patients the reality of my situation would allow me to be as analytic as possible, I can see, looking back, that telling them was also based on my need to protect myself: by telling them, I was inviting them to bring in all their feelings about what was going on with their analyst. At the same time, part of me was also asking them to temporarily suspend being the analytic patients I had asked them to be in the past and instead be reasonable adults who could understand my situation, and—at least for the next six months— have associations that were tolerable to me in my somewhat fragile emotional state.

Over time, I asked my patients their thoughts and feelings about this new reality in my life. I asked what they felt about my having secondary infertility and undergoing treatment for it. I also asked what they imagined about why I was infertile. I asked, furthermore, what they felt about my telling them the facts and what they might have felt had I *not* told them. My patients felt that these were useful analytic questions, and they responded, it seemed to me, with rich and vivid associations. I, in turn, responded to their questions with honesty, tact, and careful thought. I was pleased with my decision to disclose why I would be away so frequently. My patients and I continued to speak and listen and analyse—or so it seemed. Only months and years later was I also able to clearly understand how relieved I had been that I didn't have to deal with fantasies that I was leaving on a wonderful, spur-of-the moment vacation at a time when I was undergoing uncomfortable and sometimes painful procedures. It was only then that I could realise that part of the reason for telling my patients the reality of my situation had to do with my sense that I did not have it in me, at that point, to deal with certain reactions (e.g., rage) and fantasies (e.g., that I was going away to have "fun").

As planned, I went through two IVFs. The first did not work and my husband and I were immensely disappointed. The second was even more difficult, as it resulted in a "chemical pregnancy": The pregnancy-hormone levels rose for the first few days, creating great optimism, but then did not double as they should and ultimately fell. My husband and I were heartbroken. A chapter of our lives, we felt, had come to an end. We mourned, quietly, about what had happened and what could not happen. We spoke over the phone with our out-of-state doctor, who empathised with our sense of loss and disappointment but confirmed that this was indeed the end of the road unless we wished to pursue other kinds of treatments or perhaps adoption. Over the next few months, we discussed the other choices and finally decided that enough was enough: it was time to move on with our lives and to gratefully continue enjoying the child we had.

Little did we know that nature was planning something else for us. Five months later, on our return from a few weeks' vacation in Pakistan, we discovered that I was pregnant. Our doctor said the treatments had "primed" my system to get pregnant. I was more than happy to give everyone involved as much credit as they wanted or needed for this wonderful turn of events. My husband and I were thrilled that we would have another child and that our first child would have a sibling.

I will now share clinical material to demonstrate the fluid and changing nature of transferences that became apparent in an analysis that spanned the period of my infertility treatments, their failure, and my subsequent conception and birth of a second child.

Clinical material

Ms Lee

Ms Lee, a young African American woman and a physician, came to see me a few years after she got married. She was one of three childless patients in my practice who were struggling with primary infertility and trying to have a first child during the time that I was struggling with secondary infertility and trying to have a second child. The following sessions took place soon after my infertility treatments had failed. At which point, Ms Lee had been in analysis for five and a half years and had recently conceived, as a result of treatment for infertility.

Session 1

The patient, after lying down on the couch, talked about the fact that her coat no longer fit around her belly. She recognised that she was five minutes late again, as she had been for a few days now. She acknowledged that in the previous session, I had been wondering with her about her lateness. She added, "After the last session, I went to the maternity store, looking for maternity bras and clothes. In the dressing room, as I was trying things out, I felt very faint. I remember I felt the same when I was trying on wedding gowns before I got married. It's something about anxiety about a new life phase." After a pause, she continued. "I remember at that time, I felt bad that I was getting married, thinking about my mother, who had gotten divorced all those years ago and had never remarried." Another pause, and then she said, hesitantly, "I think I'm gloating about my pregnancy and the fact that you could not conceive. It feels awful that I have such thoughts." I asked, "Awful in what way?"

Ms Lee seemed taken aback by this. "That's a strange question," she replied, "but a good one, actually. Makes me think, if you can ask me that maybe you *don't* really think it's awful to have such gloating, mean feelings toward other people." A silence. "It's hard for me to imagine, I guess, that you might be able to understand these feelings I'm having. I'm feeling glad that I'm pregnant and you're not. That feels so mean, almost sadistic. I don't want to feel like that." I asked if she could tell me more about that. She said, "It's not *nice*," then laughed. "I know, I know, that sounds ridiculous." I said, "No, I think you're worried that *I* would find such struggles in you ridiculous. As though I couldn't possibly understand how deeply torn you feel about being so fond of me on the one hand, and having thoughts of feeling glad about my loss and suffering, on the other. You're worried that I couldn't possibly understand this is a real struggle for you and that I would laugh at you, or look down at you for being worried about not being a 'nice' person."

She replied, "When you say that, I feel perhaps you *do* understand. I felt so angry at you over all those months when you were going through infertility treatments. I thought it was so *unfair* that of all the analysts I had chosen to be with, it was you. How could I have known that you would need treatment for infertility? That's what I came to you for, for help with *my* infertility, and then lo and behold, you were going through the same problem that I was, except that you already *had* a child. I didn't even have *one*. When you were going through the treatments, I felt that your treatment was going to go really, really well, and I would never conceive. Or you would conceive before I did—that everything would be much easier for you. It's very hard for me to talk about this, but I really *needed* you, and I needed your help with my feelings about what if you had your second child and I might not even have one."

I began to better appreciate what a terrible problem Ms Lee had been—and was still—up against. During the time I was going through treatment, she had needed my help with her wish that my infertility treatments would fail and her envy about the possibility that my treatments would work and hers would not. In other words, she wanted *my* help with the hurtful and destructive wishes she had toward *me* about something she knew, *in reality*, was immensely important to me. It had seemed impossible to her, when I was in the middle of my treatment, that she could receive this much-needed help. It was only now, when I was safely (if unhappily) past that phase and she was safely and happily pregnant, that she could talk about those feelings.

I said as much to her, and she responded, "It's like asking the very person you want to hurt, to help you feel better." I said, "Exactly! Something you haven't experienced very much in your life, is it?" She started to cry. "How about not at all?" she asked after a few moments of crying. "With my mother, it's always been, 'Yes, but what about *me*?' And I have to forget about what *I* was feeling and think about how tough *her* life has been." I said, "And that's what you've been afraid of with me, that I would expect you to forget about what you're feeling and think about my problems. It's especially dangerous for you when what you want my help with is your wish to hurt me. You needed my help when you resented me and envied me, as you imagined that I might succeed with the infertility treatments and have a second child before you did."

After a momentary pause, I understood something more and added, "I think you're afraid now that as your breasts swell, and your body grows, and your coat doesn't fit because of your pregnancy, I would resent you and envy *you* as you resented and envied *me*." She responded, "Yes. I was very resentful and very envious, and to think *you* might feel like that is a frightening feeling. I don't understand how anything good can remain between us, if one of us has such feelings about the other." I said I could hear the strong worry she had about that. I could also see how good feelings between us got quite lost from her mind, when she became aware of "bad" feelings like envy and wanting to hurt me. She was truly scared that her destructive wishes had *actually* resulted in my not having conceived. "No wonder," I said, "that you feel so frightened. It all feels real to you." She admitted that it did. I then asked her about something else that had caught my ear earlier in the session; her use of the word "unfair", a word that had a history of its own in her life, with her dark skin and her many feelings and experiences (both positive and negative) connected to her skin colour. We had talked in the past about how I, with my brown skin, was "fairer" than she (an unusual experience for me in my practice), and that that was "unfair" in her mind. She associated now to my question by haltingly admitting that it felt very good to be pregnant when I was not, as though the unfairness of our different skin colours had now been righted by her having more than I did "in the pregnancy department".

Session 2

The next day, Ms Lee came in and began by telling me that she and her husband had gone for counselling regarding amniocentesis. The counsellor had described the risks of amniocentesis, and it sounded scary; they had decided not to do the procedure. "The baby is too precious," she said. "We don't want to risk losing the baby because of amnio." She then said that John's [her husband's] parents were coming the following weekend. She had not realised earlier that John would be at work at the hospital, and she would have to entertain them. She feels her mother is never there for her, but his mum is always involved in their lives. She was feeling edgy and moody, irritable at the thought of being with her in-laws, and afraid her father-in-law might say something annoying. "It's a tough time for us," she said. "Next week we're going to have some testing done."

I asked for a clarification of what the testing would be next week. She said they were going to do a very detailed ultrasound of the baby, since they had decided not to go through with amniocentesis. They would learn the baby's gender and look for other physical features to begin the process of figuring out whether the child was normal.

She said, "I wanted to keep it to myself, the fact that we will have this testing and that we'll know the gender of the baby. John had initially agreed, but now he is thinking he might tell his parents. I feel we didn't even have a chance to keep the *pregnancy* to ourselves, just as we didn't have the first dance at our wedding, and now this." I asked, "What about the first dance at your wedding?" She said, "My mother-in-law and her husband came on the dance floor right as John and I started dancing, and she blocked us from the camera so that the camera could not clearly record John and I doing our first dance. She didn't do that at her daughter's wedding, but *that* wedding, you see, she had helped plan. I didn't allow her to help me plan my wedding, so I felt that was her revenge, spoiling our first dance at our wedding. When we told them I was pregnant this time, she and my father-in-law came right over and congratulated us, but then right away she started making a fuss about having leg pain. John gave her his chair. I felt she was competing with me for attention." I asked, "From her son?" She said, "Yes—when we were on vacation in Florida recently, and we all shared a condo, she would take the chair that I wanted to sit in at the dining table. I just don't want to be around her, especially not when I'm pregnant."

I asked, "What might happen if the two of you are around each other, especially now?" She said, "She just takes things over. I don't want her answering my phone or telling me how to decorate my house. It gives me a headache. Now I'm afraid she will want to decorate the baby's room—and then John's father interrupts me when I'm talking." I said, "You sound very worried that your home, your life, your phone, your baby's room will all be taken over by them and you and John will not be able to protect your own partnership, your time, your life, your intimacy, hmm?" She said, "Yes, my feeling is that they are older; they know more about everything. They know this area much better than I do. They know all the stores. I feel they *want* us to need them and we *have* to need them because we don't know everything. I wish they needed us more. I wish we knew everything and that we had more experience, more knowledge than them so that we wouldn't need them to tell us things or show us things, because then we need them. They are not the kind of people who behave just with kindness in a helpful way. They get all puffed up and put us down and then we have to look up to them and admire them. They didn't even let John show them the movie he had made of our trip to Italy when we were together in Florida.

They just weren't interested. They are always more focused on what they've done, what they've accomplished, what they're up to."

I said, "I hear your hurt about that. And your anger. And I'm thinking that perhaps this is another feeling you had during the period of time I was going through infertility treatments, while you were also trying to conceive. That maybe you felt I was too wrapped up in myself and my needs, and too focused on what *I* could achieve and accomplish. That I wasn't able to be there for *you*. Now that I have the infertility treatments behind me, and they've failed, and I'm not pregnant, maybe *now* I'll be more interested in seeing *your* movie, and helping you with what you're feeling excited about and what *you're* worried about." She responded, "I feel selfish saying this, but I do feel that you're now more able to be here for me and not taken up with what *you* need to do. I feel as though I should apologise because that might sound very mean to you but I do feel that I have you back now, all of you, focused on me." I said, "And that's such an important feeling for you, given the lack of attention you received from your mother, who seemed depressed and preoccupied to you when you were growing up. So maybe my not being able to conceive also feels like *your* revenge on me, sort of like your mother-in-law's revenge on you, with the wedding dance." She said, thoughtfully—and with some surprise, as though she were discovering some unknown territory in herself— "Oh, I hadn't considered *that*." A silence, then, "I feel you're right. It does feel like revenge, and that feels bad, but it also feels good, sort of satisfying."

Session 3

The following session is from a year and a half further on in the analysis of Ms Lee, about five months after I delivered a baby girl who had been conceived naturally a few months after the failed infertility treatments. Ms Lee's daughter was at this time about a year old.

Ms Lee began by saying that Alyssa's (her daughter's) birthday was coming up, and she was thinking that maybe she would just have the celebration at the same time that she, her brothers, and her sister celebrated their mother's birthday. After a pause, she wondered about this decision and why she was doing this; it just seemed that it would be easier logistically. I asked, "Do you really believe that's the only reason?" She said, "I think maybe I'm trying to be more special to my mother this way, that if my daughter's birthday is celebrated along with hers, that makes me and my daughter more important on that day, compared to my other siblings." I said, "You feel you would then have a deeper connection with her than your siblings." She said, "My big gripe is my mother tries to make everything about herself, so why am I doing this? Why am I making Alyssa's birthday about my mother also?" After a quiet moment, she said, "I feel real guilty that I'm so angry at her. I have a sense I want to pay homage to her to hide how angry I am at her." I said, "I feel you're right about the guilt, because you certainly seem to be wanting to make it worse for yourself than it needs to be, by celebrating your mother's birthday along with your daughter's, rather than giving yourself the pleasure of celebrating your daughter's first birthday in a special and meaningful way. You seem to be wanting to punish yourself." She responded, "Yeah, why am I doing this on this special day that I've looked forward to for so long? Yesterday Alyssa took two steps forward. She's less interested in nursing now during the day and takes off after a couple of minutes. I will have to wean her off soon. It's painful to see her grow, much as I like it."

I said "The little baby, first flat on her back, then crawling, then standing, and now walking. Ready to take off." She said, with a catch in her voice, "I was watching this movie last night, *Butterflies Are Free*, with Goldie Hawn. She's involved with a blind guy. The guy's mother is very intrusive and controlling. He's trying to live on his own, and that's when he meets Goldie Hawn, who lives in the apartment next door. The mother finds out, and doesn't trust Goldie and wants the son to come back and live with her again. And he said okay, but he was very angry at his mother. Goldie Hawn was going to leave him, but then surprisingly, the mother encouraged him to be on his own and she said something like, 'As much as I want you to be with me so I can protect you, I need to let you go,' and he told Goldie Hawn that he was ready to be with her. So she came back to him. She had been an emotional cripple with many different fathers in her life and she kept running away from relationships." I said, "Could it be that you feel like some of the characters in this movie? Part of you feels like Goldie Hawn, a woman without a good and loving father, but you *also* feel like the blind man who was ready to go home with his mother? How poignant and wonderful that his mother could help him separate from her. He could tell her how angry he was at her and she could hear it but still have a loving relationship with him."

She seemed moved, and said, "*My* mother would feel I was killing her, if I did something like that." I said, "That could be so. Is it also possible that actually *you* might feel you *were* killing her, by not being with her?" She said, "When I hear you say that, I think about our discussions about termination and the end of our work together. Sometimes I feel I'm really crazy to think about moving on and terminating, but at other times I feel I am more and more ready. I know last year when we talked about terminating, you pointed out that I seem to be in a rush to do that, and it was at a time soon after I found out you were pregnant. I feel it was the right thing we did then, for me to postpone the termination and take more time." I said, "I agree. I feel the same. A lot of new and very useful material came up after you first brought up the idea of termination, but then settled back into analysis. It sounds, though, that you're now having a different worry about termination."

She said, "I'm really worried. I'm worried you would resent my leaving you." I said, "Yes, you're not sure if I could be a mother who might be able to help you leave me. You spoke earlier today about the bittersweet feeling as you recognise Alyssa is no longer interested in breastfeeding the way she had been. Perhaps I want to have you as my baby forever, nursing at my breast in the analysis, because of the pleasure it gives me to be able to feed you my words and my understanding of your struggles. I think you're also very afraid of being direct with me about your angry feelings." There was a long silence, and then she said, "Yes, I do feel scared you will be really offended. The truth is *I feel so competitive with you, especially since you had a second child.* All my friends are having second children now. You were able to do that naturally. I never can. I will not be able to have a second child. I feel really sad about that. I was so angry about your daughter's birth, for that reason, but that was not the only reason. It was also because I felt she replaced me. And yes, I envy you. I want to have more children than you; a nicer home than you do; to make more money than you; be more organised than you in my work and my mothering. You know what I mean?"

I said, "No, not fully. I thought you were doing very well at telling me what *you* meant, and it would be useful for us to hear more about it. But then suddenly you felt you had to stop. If *I* know what *you* mean, you don't have to go on. Is there a reason *you* don't want to tell me more about your own feelings?" She laughed nervously, and said,

"How much time do we have?" I said, "Ah, you want to condense all of this into the few minutes we have today." She said, "I wish I could, so I wouldn't have to talk about it again." I asked, "Could it be that you believe you would *really* kill me with your anger, your words, and by leaving me?"

This rich session, full of nuances and hints—the threads of which we followed over time—led to the development of a newer understanding of many of Ms Lee's conflicts: her childhood fantasies of being her mother's "man" after her parents divorced—but one who was castrated (as in the image of the blind man in the movie) for his "bad" wishes and for having done away with "his" father; her retreat to this fantasy now, at a time when her rivalrous feelings with me, feelings between two *women*, were at their peak; her fear that she would hurt me by terminating, and her wish *to* hurt me by her increasing competence; her shying away from this wish in the session by suddenly feeling she could not do the analytic work—or that we were merged and fused, rather than separate—and requiring words between us to understand what the other meant. It would be several more years before Ms Lee terminated her analysis.

Discussion

The topic of illness and disability in the analyst, and its impact on the analytic process, was rarely addressed in the early psychoanalytic literature. This is a striking omission, given that Freud, the founder of the psychoanalytic method, was severely ill with cancer during the last years of his life, and died from it. Blum (1994) writes about this:

> There was at least official, initial censorship of the possibility that Freud had a malignant neoplasm. But Freud remained extraordinarily creative during his protracted illnesses. Freud would undergo thirty-three operations prior to his death, while making major revisions and original contributions to psychoanalysis. His jaw prosthesis seriously interfered with speech, and he no longer attended congresses or gave public papers. He also developed unilateral deafness, requiring that he reverse his position in the chair. Freud did not write of the impact of his illness on himself or on his patients. (p. 874)

Blum goes on to say:

> Except for a few remarks to and by individual patients, we know
> little of the infantile conflicts and fantasies Freud's illness must
> have aroused, and the inevitable anxiety and guilt, along with the
> genuine concern that his patients must have experienced. In one of
> his letters to Marie Bonaparte, Freud apologised to her for having
> allowed his preoccupation with cancer to keep him from recognising
> a transference phenomenon in her analysis. (Ibid. p. 874).

Freud writes about his illness in personal correspondence and in his
diary, but there is no mention of it in his formal papers.

In his paper on the impact of the analyst's aging, Eissler (1977) led
the way for a reflective process, for analysts, about the effect of the analyst's functioning, both physical and mental, on his analytic work. This
was followed by Dewald's (1982) seminal paper on how transference
and countertransference might be affected by serious illness in the analyst and the kinds of responses such a situation might necessitate from
the analyst. In the years to follow, more papers on this topic entered the
analytic literature. These include Abend (1982), Anisfield (1993), Fajardo
(2001), Gervais (1994), Gurtman (1990), Halpert (1982), Kahn (2003),
Lasky (1990), Linna (2002), Rosner (1986), Strean (2002), Torrigiani and
Marzi (2005), Usher (2005), and Weinberg (1988). Schwartz and Silver
(1990) also edited a volume devoted entirely to the topic of the analyst's
illness and its implications for the therapeutic relationship.

Dewald (1982) writes:

> One important issue is the question of how much factual informa-
> tion to provide for the patients while the illness is acute. In terms
> of the future of the therapy, the more extensive the reality infor-
> mation the patient is given, the less free and uncontaminated are
> the transference distortions likely to be. Detailed reality informa-
> tion may interfere with the subsequent evolution, analysis, and
> working through of the patient's unconscious fantasies and affec-
> tive reactions to the illness. On the other hand, to leave the patient
> without factual information when there are no analytic sessions in
> which the transference implications can be brought to conscious
> awareness and ultimately analysed, may overburden the patient's
> adaptive capacity. To give extensive factual information may unnec-
> essarily allay anxiety and the occurrence of transference fantasies if

the illness turns out to be relatively benign. But to provide detailed factual information may further activate and intensify frightening fantasies if (as in my case) the illness becomes increasingly life-threatening. (pp. 349–350)

I am grateful to Dewald (1982), as a pioneer in what was hitherto an untrodden area, for writing this paper. Abend's paper (1982), another classic in this area, actually began as a discussion of Dewald's paper. I do think, however, that Dewald was being very cautious in his thinking. Over the years of working as an analyst, I have found it is simply not correct that when patients know certain realities about the analyst's life, their transferential feelings become less distorted. Significant examples of this are the visibly pregnant analyst, whose patients cannot "see" the physical evidence of pregnancy, or the analyst who has lost twenty-five pounds of weight: many of her patients could not allow themselves to "notice" what, on her small frame, was a noticeable loss. There are many similar examples. My sense is that even when patients know certain realities about the analyst, within the context of analytic work—which is aimed at working with fantasy and unconscious conflict—distortions of reality still appear, just as powerfully as if the patient knew very little about the analyst. This, then, is a remarkable testament to the power of the mind to ignore what does not suit its purposes of defence and wish fulfilment at any given moment.

Dewald (1982) also noted that the effects of the analyst's illness on patients and their analyses cannot be dealt with in a limited time span; rather, *they continue to cast a shadow over the analysis*, which must be repeatedly explored over time:

> For several patients the major effects had been worked through in the one or two months after my return, and the analysis or psychotherapy proceeded as it had before my illness. Several other patients with multiple and rigid defences against manifest dependency or affective therapeutic involvement continued to use the fact of the illness to rationalise their avoidance of transference experience and interaction. They repeatedly expressed in fantasy the anticipation of a recurrence of my illness. Any telephone call, parapraxis, cancellation of a session, or other departure by me from strict therapeutic routine activated fantasies that revolved around the possibility of my again being ill. Working through these defences is a process

that cannot be rushed and delays the resumption of a full analytic experience. Sustained analytic attention to this constellation, however, permits the eventual exposure of specific transference fantasies that underlie such characteristic defences. (p. 358)

I could not agree more with this observation.

I, too, discovered—*but only in retrospect*—that during the period I was going through infertility treatments, my patients felt a need to hold back feelings of anger or pleasure about my struggles. Though there were some expressions of frustration and anger at the disruption of the schedule, there was much greater mention of empathy and concern for me at that time. It was only in the months *after* the treatments had failed, and as I stabilised emotionally, that patients began to talk about the envy they had felt regarding the possibility that I might conceive a baby; their fear that I would be preoccupied with the baby if I had one; the anger that I was *already* preoccupied with trying to have a baby; their *pleasure* that I was struggling with something; and, finally, their ultimate pleasure and satisfaction that I had failed in what I was trying to accomplish. These more difficult feelings did not come up until *after* my infertility treatments were over, and, I suspect, until each patient felt I had dealt with my sense of loss and sadness enough that I could be relied on again to be useful to them. After that there was a period in each of the analyses I was conducting when patients allowed themselves to reflect more openly about what they had felt. They shared with me what they felt they could not have told me earlier, most of them believing that I had been too fragile then to deal with their anger about my preoccupation and their feeling glad about my struggles.

Others have written about the analyst's illness or disability having mobilised a blocked-off or arrested working through of childhood losses and trauma. Anisfield (1993) suggests:

To the degree that childhood neurosis often develops around those thoughts, impulses, and perceptions that the child deems to be unknowable, unseeable, or unspeakable, the analyst's failure to invite the patient's perceptions of his or her disability or illness in the here-and-now treatment situation constitutes the creation of still another neurosis—one that cannot, in the treatment, be resolved. What I mean by this is that there is an important distinction to be drawn between an analyst's personal revelation that is motivated by unconscious factors such as the aforementioned exhibitionism, self-protection, and so forth, and the analyst's willingness to allow the patient to speak openly about what the patient clearly senses but may be uncertain about broaching. (p. 470)

Here, the analyst's illness or disability and the patient's being informed about it—or the analyst's willingness to speak honestly when the patient notices something—is seen as a potential opportunity for the working through of feelings that had to be blocked out by the patient during childhood due to caretakers' refusal, unwillingness, or inability to deal with such matters frankly and helpfully.

About this last point, Billow (2000) cautions:

> Volitional self-disclosures should not imply that the analyst is fully aware of or certain of his or her own motivation and meanings (Aron, 1991; Frank, 1997). The rule is that there are no hard and fast rules. *One guideline is to consider whether they work to open or close things up between patient and analyst, a question that may be answered only retrospectively, and even then without certainty that another way may not have been better* (Aron, 1996a; Gerson, 1996; Greenberg, 1995; Jacobs, 1996). (p. 66; italics added)

In *Psychoanalytic Dialogues*, Buechler (2009) discusses a paper by Stuart Pizer (2009) about his experience of illness and its effect on himself and his treatment of one patient, Frank. In his commentary, Buechler writes:

> Stuart suggests that his illness forced him to lose an illusion of being in control. I think this treatment challenged Stuart to diminish reliance on mastery in several psychological as well as physical senses. [...] At first Frank insists that Stuart has all the competence, all the power, "You put all that together! Suddenly there's so much there. I couldn't do that." Stuart responds that Frank is giving himself another demerit, that he won't take any credit for his part in the creative process. Frank reiterates his usual self-belittling: "I'm no good at this. And I'm moving so slowly." But Stuart isn't buying, "And you're so wrong!" In the content and in how he behaves toward Frank, Stuart insists that we are all "little" when confronted with the vast mysteries of the unconscious and the incredible vulnerability of being human and subject to the vicissitudes of a human

body. *By healing (some of) his own need to feel in control, Stuart shows Frank that true humility is different from self-defeating, overwhelming shame. Humility faces the human condition, looks it squarely in the eye, and counters that however life tries our courage and sense of purpose, love can still do the thing that's right.* (2009 p. 67, italics added)

My own experience, and that of other analysts with whom I have discussed this issue, confirms Buechler's idea: our genuine recognition of the helplessness life confronts us with at times is often highlighted and meaningfully recognised when we face real tragedy, loss, illness, or impending mortality. And recognition of this helplessness requires giving up idealised, omnipotent fantasies of being able to control and manage one's life if one just puts one's mind to it. The analyst's hard-won recognition of this can, in turn, bring about a sharper emphasis, in the work with the patient, on the patient's unrealistic expectations of herself, others, the analyst, and even the analytic process. I find, in fact, that this is what often opens up the way to a real termination of an analysis.

Conclusion

Many of my patients carried a history of having been raised by depressed, narcissistically preoccupied, or physically ill parents who could not be available to their child, either because of serious emotional limitations or their internal anxieties. This was, then, very much part of what they were bringing into the work with me in their transferences. As I've thought about it over time, though, I believe that what we were dealing with was a collision between my patients' historical past and the current reality of their being in treatment with an analyst who *herself* was going through a difficult time in her life.

In the months during which I was undergoing infertility treatments, even though I was behaving like their usual analyst, something within me was different. I can understand, *only in retrospect*, that it was truly not possible for me, during the period when I was trying so hard—and wanted so much—to conceive a second child, to talk with my patients about their wish for me to *not* have a child, their rage that I wanted to have a child, and their worry that the child would displace them, while maintaining the same degree of neutrality, genuine curiosity, and compassion I generally had. Discussing their glee about my trials and suffering might have felt impossible then. This is an important reminder that as analysts we can ask all the right questions and say all the right things, but these come from our intellect (because of what we've learned to do, and can do, automatically), not from a place of deep emotional empathy within ourselves at that point—and our patients can sense it.

I am also aware, as I write this, of the process of useful change that occurs in an analyst, during the span of her career, as a result of continuous internal work—and experience—with both analysis and life. About ten years after my struggle with infertility, when life brought another major challenge, my ability to deal with it—and to help my patients speak about it freely in their analyses—was much greater. This will be discussed in Chapter Three.

PART II

WHEN OTHERS INTRUDE UPON CLINICAL SPACE

CHAPTER TWO

Waiting-room dramas between patients

Introduction

Although much has been written in psychoanalytic literature about the analyst's waiting room, most writing has focused on suggestions about the physical setup and arrangement of the room and its impact on the patient (e.g., Sugarman, Nemiroff, & Greenson, 1992; Goldstein, 1998; Armstrong, 2000; Hollender & Ford, 2000; Akhtar, 2009a).

Freud's writings include two descriptions of his observations about patients who expressed powerful wishes and conflicts through the way in which they negotiated their entry into his office. In the first, he writes (Freud, 1917):

> I have had the ordinary door between my waiting room and my consulting and treatment room doubled and given a baize lining. There can be no doubt about the purpose of this arrangement. Now it constantly happens that a person whom I have brought in from the waiting room omits to shut the door behind him and almost always he leaves both doors open. *As soon as I notice this I insist in a rather unfriendly tone on his or her going back and making good the omission*—even if the person concerned is a well-dressed gentleman

or a fashionable lady. This makes an impression of uncalled-for pedantry—for anyone who behaves like this and leaves the door open between a doctor's waiting room and consulting room is ill mannered and deserves an unfriendly reception. But do not take sides over this till you have heard the sequel. For this carelessness on the part of the patient only occurs when he has been alone in the waiting room and has therefore left an empty room behind him; it never happens if other people, strangers to him, have been waiting with him. In this latter case he knows quite well that it is in his interest not to be overheard while he is talking to the doctor, and he never fails to shut both the doors carefully.

Thus the patient's omission is neither accidentally nor senselessly determined and indeed it is not unimportant, for, as we shall see, it throws light on the newcomer's attitude to the doctor. The patient is one of the great multitude who have a craving for mundane authority, who wish to be dazzled and intimidated. He may have enquired on the telephone as to the hour at which he could most easily get an appointment; he had formed a picture of a crowd of people seeking for help—He now comes into an empty, and moreover extremely modestly furnished, waiting room, and is shocked. He has to make the doctor pay for the superfluous respect which he had intended to offer him: so—he omits to shut the door between the waiting room and the consulting room. What he means to say to the doctor by his conduct is: "Ah, so there's no one here and no one's likely to come while I'm here." He would behave equally impolitely and disrespectfully during the consultation if his arrogance were not given a sharp reprimand at the very beginning.

The analysis of this small symptomatic action tells you nothing you did not know before: the thesis that it was not a matter of chance but had a motive, a sense and an intention, that it had a place in an assignable mental context and that it provided information, by a small indication, of a more important mental process. *But, more than anything else, it tells you that the process thus indicated was unknown to the consciousness of the person who carried out the action, since none of the patients who left the two doors open would have been able to admit that by this omission he wanted to give evidence of his contempt. Some of them would probably have been aware of a sense of disappointment when they entered the empty waiting room; but the connection between this impression and the symptomatic action which followed certainly remained unknown to their consciousness.* (pp. 246–248, italics added).

What I find particularly interesting in this passage is the contradiction between Freud's awareness that the patient did what he did precisely because he was not consciously aware of his wishes, and that despite this understanding, Freud told the patient to go back and shut the door—as though to not do so would create a problem later in the treatment. Also, Freud considers one important possibility behind the patient's action of leaving both doors open: the patient's contempt and arrogance. He does not write about the possibility that in leaving the doors between the waiting room and the consulting room open, the patient might also be expressing a longing that no one would come after him, and that this entire space, now turned into one large, open, connected space, was only for him to be with his analyst in: a lovely and poignant wish indeed. There are other possible meanings, of course. Despite these limitations, however, I consider this passage important as an example of Freud's detailed and perceptive observation of a tiny aspect of his patient's journey from the waiting room to the consulting room.

Another significant mention of the role of the waiting room occurs in Freud's work with Dora (Freud, 1905):

> Dora's symptomatic act with the reticule did not immediately precede the dream. She started the session, which brought us the narrative of the dream with another symptomatic act. As I came into the room in which she was waiting she hurriedly concealed a letter which she was reading. I naturally asked her whom the letter was from, and at first she refused to tell me. Something then came out which was a matter of complete indifference and had no relation to the treatment. It was a letter from her grandmother, in which she begged Dora to write to her more often. I believe that Dora only wanted to play "secrets" with me, and to hint that she was on the point of allowing her secret to be torn from her by the doctor. I was then in a position to explain her antipathy to every new doctor. She was afraid lest he might arrive at the foundation of her illness, either by examining her and discovering her catarrh, or by questioning her and eliciting the fact of her addiction to bed-wetting—lest he might guess, in short, that she had masturbated. And afterwards she would speak very contemptuously of the doctor whose perspicacity she had evidently over-estimated beforehand. (p. 78)

Again, a glimpse into Freud's attention to small details, *not only about what his patients said, but also what they did—and not only in the consulting room, but also in the waiting room.*

One can tell, from most good books about setting up an analytic practice or about basic analytic technique, that psychoanalysts are quite interested in waiting rooms—but, as I mentioned before, mostly in the physical setting of the room. For instance, in *The Technique and Practice of Psychoanalysis* (Sugarman et al., 1992), Ralph Greenson writes:

> I mentioned how an experienced and apparently competent analyst had lost a good prospective patient because the patient could not bear returning to a psychoanalyst whose waiting room contained only old, stiff, rickety and straight-backed wooden chairs. I have been in that waiting room and can confirm the patient's finding. What makes the setup more disquieting is that the location of the office indicates that the analyst must have a comfortable income. I do not know this analyst well enough personally to ask him why he furnishes his waiting room and treatment room so uncomfortably and shabbily. I can only surmise from my limited personal experience, and my more extensive scientific contact with him, that his office arrangement reflects his "anti-Beverly Hills obsession" and his devotion to deeply buried psychopathology in his patients. (p. 16)

Regarding his own waiting room, Greenson writes:

> I prefer to have a waiting room large enough to seat three people comfortably, because sometimes parents will come with a child or a couple with an aging parent. There are always some current magazines for reading, usually news magazines or illustrated ones, and not only the most intellectual ones. I have one or two books of paintings or cartoons for those who have to wait for a patient whom they have to accompany to the office. (Ibid. p. 17)

With regard to patient interactions in the waiting room, Greenson remarks that patients:

> [...] seem to tolerate occasional meetings with other patients quite well as long as their reactions are brought promptly into the analytic

situation and analysed for their resistance potential. I have heard that analysts who shared a waiting room do not find their patients' reactions to other patients or analysts a formidable resistance. (Ibid. p. 17)

The reader can see here the emphasis on the arrangements and appearance of the space—and, to a much lesser degree, on what *happens* in that space.

Similarly, Hollender and Ford (2000), under the heading "The physical setting", have only this to say about the waiting room:

> The waiting room, in both the private office and the clinic setting, should afford as much privacy as possible. Rather than require the patients to sit in a circle and stare at each other, it is preferable, in large waiting areas, for the space to be subdivided either by room dividers or the arrangement of furniture. Magazines should be current. As Lewin (1965) stated, "Current magazine issues suggest that the doctor is considerate of his patients; lack of current issues implies indifference, contempt (the old ones are good enough), carelessness, or perhaps that the doctor is a slow reader." The magazines chosen often convey a subtle message about what the therapist reads or what the patient should read. (p. 13)

Again, there is no mention of any aspect of the waiting room beyond the physical setting and the arrangement of furniture, magazines, etc., within it.

In *Opening Gambits*, Peter Armstrong (2000) describes the thoughts going through his mind as he waits for a new patient to arrive:

> Gregg arrives and switches on the alert light in my waiting room. A little rush of new anxiety runs through me as it probably does Gregg. Even though I'm the therapist, I, too experience anxiety about meeting the stranger on the other side of the door. It's just a minute before the time we have set, so I go to the door hoping to convey to him that I'm ready for our meeting, and that it is important, not squeezed in between many other obligations. As I open the door I see Gregg standing there. I offer my hand for a handshake and say, "I'm Peter Armstrong." He shakes my hand and responds "I'm Gregg Williams." I motion toward my office […]. (p. 12)

Here we see a therapist aware of the partition between the two rooms, mulling over his anxiety about meeting his new patient, supposedly leaving this anxiety behind him as he crosses the threshold into the waiting room, and, with seeming ease, shakes his patient's hand.

In his book *The Use of the Self*, Ted Jacobs (1991) recounts another first meeting between analyst and patient:

> A colleague of some renown who, though large in reputation, was extremely small of stature, received a telephone call from a man who wanted a consultation. The appointment was made and at the arranged time the new patient arrived. About to enter the waiting room to greet him, the analyst suddenly stopped at the threshold and, momentarily, stood transfixed. There in front of him was a Paul Bunyan of a figure, fully six feet, eight inches in height, weighing perhaps 260 pounds and wearing cowboy boots and a ten-gallon hat. For several more seconds the analyst looked at him in silence. Then, with a shrug of his shoulders and a resigned ges-ture, he motioned toward his office. "Come on in, anyway," he said. (p. 139)

The passages I have quoted describe either the desirable physical arrangement of the waiting room or certain interactions between ana-lyst and patient in the waiting room. Some papers, particularly those that describe analytic work with children, do include minor details of what the child was doing in the waiting room, either by herself or with a parent (e.g., Caccia, 1999; Fabricius & Green, 1995; Wilson & Ryz, 1999; McDevitt, 1995). In yet a few more papers, there are descriptions of the child's forming a link between the analyst and the parent in the waiting room by means of objects taken across the threshold of the waiting room in either direction. *Very few papers have described, in significant detail, the multitude of ways patients can use the analyst's waiting room to contain, con-vey, and conceal feelings* (e.g., Freud, 1917; Kjellqvist, 1995; Kieffer, 2011), and only a handful refer to the important and complicated interactions that can develop *between patients* in the waiting room and contiguous spaces (e.g., Bergmann, 1997).

In this chapter, I will discuss the kinds of interactions that can occur *between patients* before they enter the analyst's consulting room (however brief and sporadic or detailed and sustained they might be) and the usefulness of noting these interactions.

Clinical material

Ms Smith

Ms Smith came to see me when she was almost fifty. The fourth of six children from an upper-middle-class family, she had felt emotionally neglected by both parents. The fact that her father generally behaved as though he had no time for her—and her mother seemed concerned only about school work and chores being done—made Ms Smith feel quite an unnecessary person in the world. Her only brother, who was fifth in the sibship, was doted on by both parents, while the girls were simply expected to follow rules and not cause trouble. Ms Smith resented her brother and felt disdained by her father, feelings that had deeply coloured her relationships with men in her adult life. The fact that her mother had been emotionally detached from her, and she had often felt lost among her many siblings, added to her difficulties. When she came to see me she had been through two painful relationships, was leading a rather isolated life—though she was professionally successful—and wanted to learn how she could have "a decent relationship".

Ms Smith was in the third year of a five-times-a-week analysis when she began a particular ritual. She would arrive in the waiting room of my second floor office (which was in an office building) a little more than an hour before her session and make herself comfortable. There were two chairs in the room, placed at right angles to each other, with a corner table between them. A shelf with a collection of knick-knacks ran along one wall. One door led from the outer hallway into the waiting room and another from the waiting room to an inner hallway, in which I would stand to greet my patients and bring them into my consulting room. When patients left the consulting room, they would go through this inner hallway to the outer hallway without re-entering the waiting room. Occasionally, patients would see or meet each other in the outer hallway and, more rarely, in the waiting room. As in all analyses, such chance encounters would become material in the analyses of both patients—the usual stuff of daily analytic work. Until, that is, Ms Smith introduced something more unusual and challenging.

Every day now, Ms Smith would bring her newspaper and, sitting on one of the chairs, spread it open in front of her in such a way that the patient who arrived for her regular session and took the other chair would find the newspaper almost touching her face. Ms Smith would appear to be surprised if the other patient expressed any discomfort or irritation with this arrangement. Ms Smith would arrive before the other patient and sit in the waiting room throughout that patient's analytic hour until it was time for me to bring *her* in for *her* appointment. Her presence in the waiting room at unusual times—and for prolonged periods—came to my attention both as a result of my seeing her when I opened the waiting-room door to greet the other patient and from what other patients told me.

She "explained" to me that she was arriving almost an hour early because if she drove to my office at a later time, she would have to be on the freeway during rush hour and it would take her longer. Therefore, she preferred to leave *her* office early and arrive at *my* office early, thus avoiding the rush hour on the freeway. That was how she came to have "extra time", during which she sat in my waiting room rather than in her car in the parking lot. Going to a nearby library or coffee shop seemed bothersome. Why should she do that when there was a perfectly fine space available in my waiting room?

Other patients reported that every time she turned the pages of her newspaper, they had to dodge to get out of the way; one patient said that the dreaded pages felt like "kites in the wind, smacking my face". Ms Smith had other annoying—and interesting—waiting-room rituals. From time to time, she would open a snack bag and extract something to eat, which was often an apple that she would vigorously and noisily chomp on. After it had been eaten to the core, she would throw it into the wastebasket, which was some distance from her chair. Sometimes this resulted in the core landing on the carpet—where Ms Smith, quite unconcerned, would leave it, much to my other patients' outrage. "She's littering up the place!" another patient exclaimed, "like she's some fucking queen of nowhere. Who does she think is going to pick up that mess?" Apparently, at some point during her sojourn in the waiting room, Ms Smith *would* get up and deposit the core into the wastebasket—but not until she had made her point: that she could throw things around there, and she would pick them up only when she was good and ready.

Initially, my other patients—though feeling intruded upon—were curious and mildly amused; they thought this was something temporary. However, when Ms Smith's behaviour continued day after day, week after week, they were no longer amused: why wasn't I doing anything about this? they wondered. Why didn't I *tell* her to stop doing this? I, in turn, felt intrigued, puzzled, and annoyed by Ms Smith's behaviour—and, indeed, by her. On one hand, I felt concerned for my other patients and the violation of their time and space in the waiting room. On the other hand, I felt defensive: I *had* been talking to Ms Smith about what she was doing in the waiting room and what it might mean. What did my other patients expect me to do? After all, I couldn't force her to stop; that did not feel analytically useful to me. Gradually, I began to have the sense that I had been put in a position of having to be the "analytic mother of many," trying to juggle my various patients and wanting to do right by each, but feeling rather ineffective. I now began to discuss this with Ms Smith, wondering about the link between the scenario she had created and her childhood home, where she had had to vie with her siblings for her mother's attention.

Ms Smith was politely interested in my observation about the connection between her childhood life as one of many siblings and her behaviour in the waiting room with my other patients. I was "rewarded" for this interpretation by Ms Smith's addition of yet another dimension to her waiting-room drama: she continued to arrive early, but then, from time to time during her wait, she would go into the outer hallway, either to get a drink of water or to use the restroom. This meant that in my consulting room, I was frequently confused by the sound of the waiting-room door opening and closing. Since Ms Smith was arriving more than an hour before her session, when I heard the waiting-room door open the first time, I would wonder whether it was Ms Smith or the patient whose appointment preceded hers. I would therefore open my consulting-room door, go into the inner hallway of the office suite, open the waiting-room door, and peer into the waiting room. There I would find Ms Smith ensconced in her chair, the newspaper spread before her, eating an apple quite cheerfully. She would peek at me around the newspaper and either smile and say, "It's just me," or—realising that I was looking for the other patient—shake her head slightly and say, "Nope—isn't here yet." I would then go back to my office, only to hear the outer door of the waiting room open and close again a few minutes later, and the whole drama would then be repeated.

Patients reported to me that when they arrived in the waiting room, Ms Smith would usually tell them that I had been looking for them and that she had informed me they had not yet arrived. Ms Smith was thus able to monitor my other patients' comings and goings—while also confusing me and making it necessary for me to repeatedly leave the consulting room and check to see whether the patient I was *supposed* to see had just arrived. My other patients were now openly angry with Ms Smith. They considered her to be offensive, intrusive, and intimidating and wondered how she could, ostensibly, be oblivious to her effect on them and her disturbance of a usually calm, empty waiting room. They wanted me to put an end to her behaviour and wondered why I did not forbid her from doing this.

With each patient who had been affected by Ms Smith's uninvited establishment of a private kingdom in the waiting room, I acknowledged that this was indeed an unusual and difficult situation for them to contend with. I also tried to explore what this difficult situation brought up for each of them. Patients often associated to the idea of Ms Smith as an intrusive, self-absorbed parent or a sibling who was bossy, got preferential treatment, and was allowed to get away with bad behaviour. I was seen as either favouring Ms Smith, being afraid of her, or not caring about my other patients. In contrast, my efforts to interest Ms Smith in looking at the meanings of her actions did not lead to much success at this point. I felt guilty about not being able to protect my other patients from her intrusions and incompetent because I could not help Ms Smith understand why she was doing what she was doing or stop it.

Weeks went by. Ms Smith, my other patients, and I were now all part of an established, problematic ritual, each of us seemingly helpless to change the situation we were in, as though we were resigned to—and locked into—this unhappy state of affairs. At this point I found myself dreading the sounds of Ms Smith's premature arrivals in the waiting room. The repetitive confusion I had to deal with, as I wondered whether it was "just" her or another patient I needed to bring into the consulting room, was beginning to wear me down. I felt irritated and angry with Ms Smith. I felt resentful that I had to deal with the fallout created by her behaviour, both as it affected me and as it affected my other patients. Every day, when it was time for Ms Smith's arrival, I felt these feelings wash over me. And gradually, through the haze of my discomfort, anger, and sense of helplessness and incompetence, I began to wonder about my feelings and what I could learn from them. Levine and Brown (2013), in their editors' introduction to a paper by Raul Hartke, write:

> In every analysis, there is a shared powerful emotional experience that patient and analyst must face together and that inevitably touches upon areas of their individual personalities. The turbulence

that follows from this individual and/or mutual evolution [...] produces "a sort of psychic vertigo" or existential encounter with what is truly alien and unknown in one's emotional experience and in oneself. (p. 129)

In the midst of my own "psychic vertigo," I began now to connect my current experiences with Ms Smith to my own life history. What I thought about were not new facts, but the feelings connected to these facts came up in a more genuine, powerful, and experience-near way. I thought about the birth of my younger brother, my ambivalent feelings about him, my memories of being displaced, my struggles to feel special in my family, my childhood wishes to scare or annoy my baby brother during those early years, and the major changes that occurred in me and my family soon after his birth—changes that, with a child's unreasonable logic, I ascribed to his birth. And I thought of much, much more. Perhaps the most important aspect was that I felt freer to truly think analytically about this issue in a more spontaneous and real way. I also became aware that my earlier comments to her about what she was doing and what it might mean had been somewhat rote, premature, annoyed, and not affectively attuned to her distress because I had not yet linked them, in my mind, to memories of distressing times in my own life. Jacobs (1991) writes:

> The importance of the patient's memories is well known. Perhaps less well recognised is the importance of the analyst's memories. Blum (1980) has pointed out that reconstruction of the patient's childhood is often accompanied by reconstruction of the analyst's childhood, and that these are independent, if overlapping, processes. [...] It is through his own memories and the affects connected with them that, in large measure, he understands his patient's inner experiences. [...] For the analyst to be truly empathic, his own memories must be available to him. This is one of the most important effects of the analyst's own analysis. [...] When shifted into a mobile state, these memories are then free to rise up to meet those of the patient. (pp. 131–132)

This is what I felt was now happening. And as my mind slowly came out of a state of feeling analytically paralysed and overburdened, I began to feel a sense of renewed hope that Ms Smith and I might be able to understand what she was trying to remember—and to share with me—through the waiting-room scenario she had created.

Over the next few weeks, I began to address the issue more directly and somewhat differently in the analysis. I said to Ms Smith that though she continued to feel there was nothing much to be understood by her behaviour in the waiting room, I was starting to realise that this might be her way of remembering and trying to describe something to me that had been a chronic, and very painful, situation in her life—something that she was not fully in touch with yet. I thought it might be useful for me to gather together, in words, what I observed her doing in the waiting room, her interactions with other patients, and her interactions with me while she sat in the waiting room. I then described how I saw her early arrival in the waiting room as giving her an opportunity to be the first one there, who could keep an eye on others who were coming and going. Her comments to other patients about my "looking for them" established her as the one who knew all about whom I was waiting for and the main link between me and others who wished to be with me. At the same time, she could see the effect on me of her early arrival and then her repeated comings and goings between the hallway and the waiting room: each time, I had to get up and see who was in the waiting room and whether or not I needed to bring someone in from the waiting room. I also spoke about her comments to me regarding other patients who had not yet arrived, again establishing herself as an authority about people I was waiting for—*those yet to come*. I told her I wanted to make it clear that in my experience with such actions in an analysis, nothing much was ever gained by the action's simply being stopped without also being understood. My hope, I told her, was that both of us might now be in a better position to understand what was going on: she would be helped the most by trying to understand what this might mean and my feeling was that she, herself, did not yet understand it.

Ms Smith listened intently and seriously. Her first response was one of feeling embarrassed, accused, and criticised. I asked about those feelings in light of what I had specifically said to her, and she said that it reminded her of many, many times in her childhood when she had been told that something she was doing was wrong and she should just stop doing it. She added that at the same time, she also "knew" I was not suggesting the she stop doing what she was doing immediately, nor did she feel she wanted to or could. Part of her still felt that she had arrived at what she was doing and the way she was doing it because it really did make more sense for her logistically. As she heard me describe what I saw happening between the two of us, however, and between her and other patients in the waiting room, *she felt, for the first time, intrigued by and curious about her own behaviour.*

I shared with her that I felt heartened, and glad for her, that she could feel this sense of curiosity about her own actions. I believe strongly that helping a patient become curious about their own feelings and behaviours is half the task of an analysis: as the adult patient rediscovers the sense of curiosity about herself and others, which is such an innate part of a good-enough childhood (and which gets suppressed along the way due to internal and external injunctions, shame, fear, and other factors), the analyst finds a true collaborator in the joint work of analysis. Both partners in the analytic dyad then have the same goal: they are both curious about what is going on in the patient's mind, why, and what to do with and about it. I felt, for the first time, that Ms Smith and I were approaching this level of curiosity and collaboration about the waiting-room dramas within which she was enacting and embroiling me and the other patients.

Clearer associations now came up about what Ms Smith was trying to achieve by establishing her domain in the waiting room. She said she realised that she and my other patients were "like sisters and brothers." Life for her with her sisters and her baby brother had not been easy. "My parents had no time for me," she reflected sadly. "That seemed to be the most precious commodity. That, and affection. Everything was spread so thin, with six of us born over nine years. It's like we were always grabbing, vying for attention." Understanding more now, I ventured, "So when you come here long before your session, you are getting more time than any of my other patients. You have essentially two sessions every day: one in the waiting room and one when you come into my consulting room. Perhaps it's a way of finally receiving the gift of time you should have received, as a kid, now from me, but through being in my waiting room—because the actual session is so strictly limited to forty-five minutes." She said, "I hate that—every time you say we need to stop, I hate it. Then you go see someone else."

She recalled, tearfully, how limited her mother's time and love felt to her, and how lost she felt amid the needs and demands of so many other siblings. This became even more marked after the birth of her baby brother, who was treated by her parents and some of her older sisters as God's gift to the family and, indeed, to mankind. In talking more about this, it became clearer that, through her waiting-room drama, Ms Smith was also trying to reverse the inferior and insignificant status she felt she had in her family by becoming my "most important patient." She was able, over time, to acknowledge, poignantly, that she could see she had turned herself into my indispensable secretary. Sitting in the waiting room for hours also allowed her to see very clearly who was coming and going, something that she had had no control over in her family of origin. Nobody had asked her which, if any, siblings she wanted to have. Sitting in the waiting room, however, she could keep an eye on who was leaving, since she often ran into the exiting patient in the outer hallway as she went to get water or visit the bathroom, and she could see very clearly who was arriving in the hour before her session. It gave her a sense of control and importance. She was able to acknowledge, with a pang of horrified recognition, that she had a wish to "torture" me by making me repeatedly wonder who was in the waiting room and have to go out and check. This was my punishment for being with her analytic "siblings." At the same time, it made it much easier for her to have a direct and problematic impact on the other patients, making them feel as uncomfortable and unneeded as she had felt in her family.

Exploration of these feelings finally allowed us to investigate the meaning of her eating in the waiting room—and particularly apples, which was what she seemed to eat the most frequently in the waiting room—and the core that was then thrown into (or, more likely, *at*) the wastebasket. Multiple aspects of this came up in the association. One of her first thoughts was the trouble the apple had caused in the garden of Eden, indicating both her sexual longings for me but also her terror that she would be extruded and pushed out of my practice if she did not stop her bad behaviour—that she would lose her garden of Eden with me because of this irritating behaviour. Most painfully, she felt that the apple core that was being deposited in the wastebasket represented in her mind a part of herself, "the bad seed" she felt she had been treated as, in her family, particularly during her teenage years, when she would often get drunk with friends, come home late, and get into trouble with her parents. She felt that no one understood that she was doing that in part because she wanted attention—any kind of attention—from her parents, but felt instead that in the midst of so many siblings she was often simply a wasted apple core, "like a piece of shit," that was being relegated to the wastebasket.

This led to an opening up of very painful and negative feelings about herself, which were being managed, in part, through her omnipotent, seemingly unconcerned, and controlling behaviour in the waiting room. Very gradually, about six or seven months after her waiting-room ritual had begun, she decided she would either leave her office later and arrive in time for her session or, if she arrived an hour before her session, she would read at a coffee shop close by. Much later in the analysis, we revisited these waiting-room sequences in the context of Ms Smith's description of occasionally hearing sounds from her parents' bedroom, which she later connected with lovemaking, and her childhood curiosity about what was going on behind closed doors that she was not privy to.

Mr Murray

Mr Murray was in his fifties and had never had any treatment before; he came to see me complaining of dissatisfaction with his personal life. He had dated a number of women during his life, but had never been able to develop a truly meaningful, intimate relationship. He had recently retired from his position as a successful executive, and found himself at loose ends. He was wondering whether he should do long-term contractual work with the company he had retired from, or go into business for himself. After hearing his history, I recommended analysis, since it seemed to me that this would be the best way for us to understand his many different conflicts. He felt he was neither interested in nor ready to do that, however, and decided instead to begin at a once-a-week frequency. Soon thereafter there were associations in his sessions that suggested he was worried about "a mess" being created in the analysis, and as we analysed this fear, he decided that he wanted to start coming twice a week, but remain sitting up.

At this point, I had moved my office from the office building I had been in to an office suite that been added onto my home. Patients would come into the main foyer of the office suite, from which they could enter the waiting room. The inner door of the waiting room opened into a short hallway, from which doors led into my consulting room and the bathroom. There was also a water dispenser in this hallway. The waiting room was furnished with a couch, a long, freestanding display shelf, and a table for magazines.

Sometime after we started working together at a twice-weekly frequency, I opened the waiting-room door to find Mr Murray lying on the couch in my waiting room, a couple of pillows behind his back. He sprang up guiltily as I opened the door, as though I had caught him doing something he should not have been doing. As we talked about it in the session that day, he noted that he had done that a few times in the past, but had been afraid that I might see him lying on the couch. I asked what he was afraid of, and he said that it felt so comfortable to him, he was worried that he might fall asleep; he might cuddle into it as he used to on the couch in the den of his family home when he was growing up.

I said, "Could it be you're worried about that happening in here, if you were ever to use the couch in my consulting room?" He acknowledged that he was indeed worried that he might fall asleep on the couch in my office. Then he added with a half laugh that perhaps he was more worried he might *not* fall asleep: what if he stayed awake and realised that he liked it? I asked, "So, what then?" This led to a whole series of associations about his fear of becoming too dependent on others in relationships, and his worry that as his dependence on the other person was exposed, they would find him to be too much. "Like a burden," I said, "rather than your need to be understood by the other person, and accepted." He said that *that* made him feel understood.

A number of weeks ensued during which Mr Murray would routinely stretch out on the couch in my waiting room prior to his sessions and read a magazine, and would then get up—but without much embarrassment, guilt, or shame—when I opened the waiting-room door. It was as though he was "trying out" the couch in the waiting room, and I said as much to him. The time he spent in the waiting room then gradually increased over time, going from a few minutes to twenty to twenty-five minutes. I now noticed with him that the length of his solitary sessions on the couch in the waiting room had increased. He was able to consider this and acknowledge that perhaps he was "testing out" the couch. This eventually led to his beginning to want to use the couch in my office, stating that he felt less worried about it now, and gradually moving from twice-weekly frequency to four times a week on the couch. His longer time in the waiting room vanished soon after this frequency was established.

Very early in the analysis, Mr Murray began talking about his parents' difficult and messy divorce when he was about seven years old. The parents had had joint custody of Mr Murray and his younger brother, and the children were shuttled between their parents, who soon had new partners and stepchildren. He recalled, painfully and with great emotion, how difficult this arrangement had felt to him. At this point in the treatment, he again started to arrive a little early for his session. However, he no longer used this time to sit or lie down in the waiting room. Instead, he would use the bathroom in my office suite every time he came. Upon departure, Mr Murray would go back into the main foyer (from which patients entered the office suite from outside) and wait there until the next patient had left the waiting room. Then he would re-enter the waiting room and cross through to the water dispenser on the inner hallway, where he would take a paper cup, fill it with water, and return to his car. Every single time. Despite his seemingly careful and thoughtful plan to not intrude on a patient who might be waiting for me in the waiting room, his journey through the waiting room to the water dispenser and back through the waiting room often led him to a patient in the waiting room, either on his way in or his way out.

The other patients began to speak about this problem in their sessions; they didn't like it, and wondered why he had to do it every single time: why didn't he just bring his own water, or take more water at the beginning of his session, so that he could "take himself and his fucking water" (in the words of one patient) right out the door after his session? As I became aware of this pattern, I began to talk with him about it, wondering what it might mean. He initially rationalised the entire ritual, saying that he had to use the bathroom each time because he came from some distance and that he took the cup of water from the water dispenser because he needed to take a thyroid supplement every day, and he had decided he would take it after his session every day so that he wouldn't forget.

We gradually understood that the ritual performed outside the consulting room contained a whole host of feelings. It had to do with having access to, and being able to use all the spaces in my office suite: the bathroom, the foyer, the waiting room, the consulting room, and the alcove that contained the water dispenser. In Mr Murray's mind, his repetitive wanderings in all the parts of my office suite, both before and after his session, were like the reversal of his childhood reality: the inaccessibility of the two parental homes he vacillated between, where the parents' subsequent partners had children whose bedrooms, bathrooms, and certain play areas Mr Murray and his brother were denied access to.

It was also a way of depositing his mess in my bathroom, thus laying primary claim to it, and marking it as his territory for all the other patients to know (he would often leave the toilet paper trailing on the floor behind him or paper towels that had missed the mark when he threw them into the wastepaper basket). This would then be cleaned up, either by me or another patient.

A brief interaction with my young daughter helped me better understand another aspect of Mr Murray's feelings and to bring them to his attention in a language he readily connected with. My daughter, who was then about four years old, would often come to my office suite in the late evening when all the doors would be open and I might be doing some paperwork in the back room. She would go to the water dispenser and get a cup of water to drink. One day, after drinking the water, she declared, "This is the most drinky water in the whole world!" In that moment, I understood what my patient was trying to deal with by taking this water with him as he left my office. I could then begin to talk with him about his feeling that all his life, he had felt short of certain supplies—as expressed in the idea of having a thyroid deficiency—because of the choppy, and at times neglectful, parenting he had received. Therefore, he had to take this "most drinky water in the world" from my office to sustain him while we were separated. His doubts about ever being able to feel genuinely special and loved (the same doubts that got him in trouble with girl-friends) gradually came into the analysis as the years went by—and words, expressing feelings, took the place of his waiting-room and water-dispenser dramas.

Discussion

The threshold between the waiting room and the consulting room is a significant boundary, with important meanings. Berman (1950), for instance, writes:

> Certain rather familiar observations in analysis show that subjec-
> tively *the patient frequently experiences the walls of the analyst's office as
> being semi-permeable*. There are chance meetings with other patients,
> real or imagined, perception of a warmed-up couch from the pre-
> ceding patient, cigarette stubs in waiting room ash trays, the ana-
> lyst's secretary, etc. Some of these experiences remain uncathected
> in the analysis, while others may become important parts of the

analytic situation. For example, *significant infantile rivalry constellations both as regards oedipal and sibling jealousies may be activated by these real experiences contiguous to the therapeutic situation.* Thus, although in group psychotherapy a number of individuals are spatially and temporally contiguous during the actual therapeutic session, it may be seen that *in psychoanalysis, in connection with the patient's experience of the unsharp boundaries of the analyst's office and the timelessness of the unconscious, the patient may react to the analytic situation as if there were more than two individuals present.* (p. 158, italics added)

In the vignettes from my own practice, two patients used the semipermeable walls—and, in Berman's words, "the unsharp boundaries" of the analyst's office—to construct dramas in the waiting room between themselves and other patients, to learn something about themselves, and to convey it to the analyst.

In her paper "On siblings: Mutual regulation and mutual recognition" (2008), Kieffer writes:

> It must be remembered that sibling transferences in child and adolescent patients are significantly different from those of adult patients. In work with children, material about sibling relationships is quite prominent from the very beginning of the analysis, with elder siblings tending to complain about younger ones intruding into their space and younger ones complaining about mistreatment by their older siblings. In some cases, these experiences may follow them into the consultation room: Lana, a shy six-year-old analysand, frequently complained of bullying by her three-years-older brother, Rob. About six months after the analysis began, Rob, who often accompanied Lana and her mother to my office, made numerous attempts to enter my consultation room, much to his sister's distress and my consternation and puzzlement as I identified with my young patient's experience of being taunted and impinged upon. (p. 168)

Kieffer goes on to say:

> Another of my analytic patients, Carla, had been increasingly resentful of a profoundly autistic brother, Joey, who often invaded this thirteen-year-old girl's bedroom and tore up her things,

including treasured pictures of pop idols and clothes. Carla started analysis feeling markedly guarded about revealing her internal world, displaying a fierce form of protectiveness that had seemed evocative of her struggles to keep her chaos-inducing younger brother out of her teenaged sanctuary. Much of the early material was focused on Carla's resentment of her brother and her wish to destroy him, with empathic ruptures often sending my patient into the waiting room to "keep me out" of her world. During this phase, I interpreted to Carla that she might experience me as another unwelcome intruder who might disrupt her inner world with chaos and other forms of damage; she replied by telling me that she was deliberately trying to make herself so impossible that I would "just go away," as she wished Joey would do. (Ibid. p. 169)

In adult analysis, we often hear about our patients' rivalries, jealousies, and conflicts about their siblings. It is well known that the analyst's other patients become a vehicle through which such rivalries are expressed in the transference—closer to home, and in a more experience-near way. And sometimes these conflicts present even more flagrantly, as with Ms Smith and Mr Murray.

The most painful aspects of one's past—and the most shameful longings—need to be kept private, even from oneself. Such is the demand of the need for survival during a tough childhood. When such feelings and longings are reactivated during an analytic treatment, it is often not possible for patients to feel them, take ownership of them, or express them directly. And yet they push for expression, as the high frequency of analytic meetings provides both the safety and the intensity for such feelings to emerge—which is an analytic treasure, since it allows for more detailed working through of the long-denied wishes and conflicts that surround them. Yet, given the pain and shame associated with such desires and feelings, they are often expressed indirectly and, as in the clinical examples above, in a way designed to camouflage the problem. Faced, on the one hand, with the wish to express and on the other with the wish to conceal, *certain memories and feelings are then expressed in a way that allows hope both for concealment and discovery*. In such instances, when the mind uses all possible mechanisms at its disposal, the threshold between the analyst's waiting room and consulting room becomes a helpful boundary of advance and retreat for the patient. It creates an illusion that what happens in the waiting room will stay in the waiting room, and is not really a part of the analysis. At the same time, by involving other patients in a waiting-room drama, the patient is not only playing out sibling and oedipal rivalries, but is also ensuring that word about what's going on in the waiting room will get to the analyst.

Gabbard's "The exit line: Heightened transference–countertransference manifestations at the end of the hour" (1982) is helpful in this regard, since it refers to the same phenomenon. He writes:

> The exit line is stated while leaving precisely because the patient wants to keep it out of the session. More exactly, the patient is ambivalent about communicating this material in his sessions. Hurling it as a parting shot is a compromise between saying it and not saying it. The communication is often so emotionally charged that it can only be conveyed to the analyst as the session ends, where a breather from the situation will follow. Freud (1913) noted that some patients, who object to lying down, view these final comments as separate from the formal treatment process. *He advises the analyst not to accept this artificial separation.* (p. 580, italics added)

Similarly, with regard to waiting-room dramas, it is helpful to be mindful of what these interactions between patients in a space separated from—yet connected to—our offices are designed to convey. As Gabbard points out, such explorations often tap into a rich vein of emotional gold.

Beyond the waiting room, as patients leave our offices, there is, of course, a whole other world of people who affect the analytic process in different ways. In the next chapter I will explore this impact, focusing specifically on the issue of patients who hear from other people about their analyst's personal life and the complex feelings this brings into the analysis.

CHAPTER THREE

"Have you heard?" Revelations regarding the analyst

Introduction

An issue that has rarely been addressed in the psychoanalytic literature is that of patients hearing from others about issues in the analyst's personal life or aspects of the analyst's personal or professional functioning. While searching the PEP (psychoanalytic electronic publishing) database, I tried various approaches, including "patients discussing their analysts" and "patients learning about their analysts from others," which came up empty. "The analyst's personal life" yielded a handful of articles—but none that specifically dealt with patients who were in treatment hearing, from someone else, something about their analyst. Finally, I searched for "gossip about the analyst" and retrieved several useful papers that discussed this possibility.

The authors of these papers (which will be discussed later in the chapter) acknowledge that this is inevitable, caution the analyst about revealing too much, and suggest, wisely, that such "revelations" shared with the analyst regarding what has been "revealed" to the patient by others should be dealt with in the same way one deals with all analytic material. Other important aspects were largely ignored, however, such as how such knowledge gained from others might come up in a treatment and function to help or hinder the analysis. The only exception to this approach is Phillips's 1998 paper, which I will discuss later.

The relative lack of such details in our literature raises many questions. We often read papers or hear material in which patients discuss the wonderful attributes they ascribe to their analysts and their envy of the analyst's "good life". Why is so little written about patients' discovery of *difficulties* in the analyst's life, such as divorce, problems with children, personality traits that others complain about, and "secrets" about the analyst's earlier life? One would think, from a review of the literature, that analysts never encounter these problems, and that therefore these problems cannot be heard about by their patients. This is obviously not true. Living in the communities we do, and doing the work we do, each of us knows that our patients are discussing among themselves—and with others in the community—the latest upheavals, major and minor, in their analysts' lives. Word gets around quickly in the analytic community, as it does in all others. And that is as it should be: it's part of being human.

In response to an inquiry about this topic I posted on the American Psychoanalytic Association's members' listserv in June 2013, a number of colleagues shared, via telephone and email, anecdotes from their own work. Even so, analysts rarely write about such matters and the difficult feelings that can be evoked in both analyst and patient, the clinical complexities, and the possibilities for growth (on both sides of the couch) they introduce.

This chapter addresses clinical issues in working with patients who have heard, from others, something about their analyst. In contrast to the situation I described in Chapter One, in which I decided to share certain information with my patients, here I address events in my personal life that I did not feel I needed to inform my patients of. Although the events caused a profound emotional upheaval I needed to work on within myself—and, as such, would necessarily affect my work from time to time—they did not have a direct or disruptive impact on the frame of the treatments I was conducting. These were not secret; my husband and I discussed them, as appropriate, with family, friends, and colleagues. In regard to patients, however, I felt it was best to simply wait until they either heard about them or found out in some other way. At that point, I hoped, we would deal with what had happened/was happening in my life, both as a current reality and in terms of what it evoked in them.

The series of events had to do with my older child being transgendered, and—with the support of family and various professionals—going through the medical/surgical/legal stages of a young adult's transition from female to male. This took place when I had been in the analytic profession for about eighteen years.

I will use clinical vignettes from my work with two patients to illustrate how patients reported hearing about this change in my life, what their reactions were, how I felt and responded, and how this became part of the tapestry of our analytic exploration of their inner worlds. *The clinical interactions described in the first vignette occurred about two years before those of the second vignette. As such, the two vignettes—in addition to highlighting my patients' different responses—also demonstrate the changes, over time, in my own emotional state and functioning.*

Clinical material

Mr Martin

Mr Martin, who had been in analysis with me for six years, had emigrated to America from Argentina as a young man, ostensibly because he was sponsored for a visa by a firm that valued his professional expertise. Over time we learned that he had, in fact, left his country—his "motherland"—because of extreme bitterness toward both his parents, and particularly his mother; he felt that she had never understood or loved him. He felt that she cherished his sisters and, as he put it, seemed "to love girls best". She valued his older brother, it seemed to him, because he resembled her mother (his grandmother)—while Mr Martin, in contrast, had been an unwanted and unplanned fourth child, seven years younger than his older sister.

He described his mother as a woman who had had to give up her own higher education, after her father died at a young age, to go to work and help her mother support her younger siblings, who were all boys. Mr Martin's father was a professional who made a decent living, but had always been treated by his wife as though he hadn't quite succeeded in life. Mr Martin remembered many heated conversations between his parents, during which his mother would attempt to get his father to accept her suggestions about how to market his business and make more money. His father would seem ashamed but try to be nonchalant, saying he didn't *want* to make more money and was happy with how his business was doing. Mr Martin recalled feeling very angry at—and sorry for—his mother, and enraged at his father for not standing up to his mother. He felt his father was "so beaten" by his mother, and perhaps also depressed, that he had never been able to attend to his young son's emotional needs.

Mr Martin grew up to be a successful professional and did quite well financially, but could not find happiness with a woman. He came to see me when he was in his forties, having gone through two failed marriages and one engagement that had been broken off by his fiancée, who felt that he was suspicious, controlling, and too focused on himself. Our analytic work was remarkable for his consistent and powerful doubts about my having any genuine interest in him. This might fade from view for a short while, but would quickly resurface. Even as we seemingly worked together to understand his pain about having felt devalued by his mother—and ignored and unsupported by his father—I realised, over time, that we were skimming the surface while a critical basic problem remained virtually untouched: Mr Martin's essential doubt that he could ever be genuinely loved by anyone.

One day in the sixth year of his analysis, Mr Martin told me that he had heard from a friend of his—who was married to a psychologist—that my older child was transgendered: my daughter was now my son. The news, he said, had come from a reliable source and did not surprise him much. This, stated quite calmly, surprised *me*; it was not at all most people's usual response. "Yes?" I managed to ask, temporarily swallowing my surprise at his calm reaction.

He paused, then said, "Yes, I know these things happen. In Argentina, I knew a couple of people who were transgendered. It's more common now than ever before, because it's easier for people to come out, talk about it. I would think you helped your daughter through all of it. At least, I hope so."

There was a pause, during which I found myself thinking back over the last several months. My daughter's transition, with its many aspects, was still relatively new; my husband and I, and our daughter and her younger sister, were still in the throes of dealing with our changed reality. We each mourned what we thought we had had, and what we had now lost; welcomed what was new, while trying to adapt to it; were relieved that our child was no longer suffering, but shaken by the gravity of what we had learned. Most important of all, we were grateful to be moving through this passage together, connected by love that had grown steadily stronger.

Sitting behind Mr Martin, my eyes filled with tears as I thought, yet again, of the pain I felt my former daughter had endured, the struggles I imagined my new son was now dealing with as he strived to feel more at home in the world, and the complex feelings my husband and I—and our younger child—were still struggling with. After a few moments, Mr Martin spoke again. "Yes, for me," he said, "it's not a surprise that you have a transgendered child. What I don't understand is why you didn't know from the time your daughter was a little girl." Emerging from my sense of grief, I felt a bit stunned by this. I recalled the doubts I had had about myself after our daughter came out to us as being transgendered: what had I done wrong, what had I missed, how could I have prevented this? These were doubts I was gradually coming to understand as having deep roots in earlier events of my life, events that, in my most powerful and painful fantasies, I believed I had caused or been responsible for. Now Mr Martin was raising a new question for me to consider: should I have somehow known, from the time my child was very young, that she was transgendered?

I attempted to gather my thoughts, then asked him, "So, what do you think? *How come* I didn't know, from the time she was little?" He sniffed, as though he had just smelled something offensive, and replied, "Well, to me, that just confirms my worst misgivings about you. You obviously don't listen. And you don't understand. That's what I often tell you. If you were capable of understanding, you would have understood this about your daughter a long time ago. It's as simple as that: a girl feels more comfortable being a boy. What's to not understand about that? Where's the complication?"

His voice rose as his rage increased. "What took you so long to get it? That just sounds to me like something that's typical of you. You're not interested in really listening, so you don't really understand. I'm telling you, *you just missed the boat*, that's what it is, you *missed* the boat on this with your kid." I felt, for a moment, pained and outraged. His statement that things were very simple, and that sometimes a girl just feels more comfortable being a boy—though true in a certain way—seemed, at the same time, to strip things down, in a highly reductionist way, to some basic facts that had, purportedly, escaped my attention. This, in turn—in his view—had caused further harm to my child. The more I mulled his accusations in my mind, the more I began to wonder what, for him, all of this was about.

I was able then to reflect with him, "You feel that, if only I had been able to listen and understand better, I would have known, from the very early years of my daughter's life, that I had a transgendered child. The problem lies in my not doing so. And I wonder what you imagine about that? What would have prevented me from listening, and wanting to understand?" I thought Mr Martin might say that my anxiety and fear about knowing the truth might have made me deny certain things, or that my need to maintain my lovely daughter in the image I was familiar with, and loved, made it difficult for me to face the truth—or even that my shame about having a child who was "different" and my guilt about imagined wrongdoing on my part made me cling to the status quo.

Instead Mr Martin said, slowly and bitterly, "I think there's something missing in you. You're just not capable of doing it. Maybe you want to, but you just can't." Now I was intrigued. "You mean," I asked, "that there is something inherently limited in terms of my capacity to really listen and understand?" He nodded vigorously. "Yes, exactly!" "In that case, then," I asked, thinking harder now, "whatever I do, I can't change that aspect of myself, right? It's inherent. Maybe women can change into men, and men into women, but my limited capacity to truly listen and understand is so intrinsically a part of me that it cannot be changed. So my daughter—now my son—*and* you are stuck with me and stuck with this problem in me."

Mr Martin shifted on the couch, and I could see his body relax a little. He seemed to be taking in what I had just said and thinking about it. "That's right," he said. "It makes me feel hopeless about *us*, and the possibility of this analysis ever really helping me fully. I feel you are like a mechanical analyst, you understand things brilliantly, but you don't really get it. You don't, and can't really, get me emotionally."

I felt his distress, his sense of helplessness, and the disappointment and fear behind his fierce, attacking words. I said, "I can imagine how awful it feels to have me as your analyst, when you feel so hopeless about my ability to truly connect with you emotionally, to know you, and to understand you as you wish to be known and understood." In response, Mr Martin reverted to feeling resentful and said, sarcastically, "You got *that* right, Doc!" I realised that it was a problem for him when

I didn't understand him—but it seemed to be just as much, if not more, of a problem when I *did* get what he was feeling. I felt we'd have to wait and see where this led us.

After he left, I found myself thinking a lot about what had (and had not) transpired between us, wondering about all he had been trying to tell me and what I had not understood. I knew that his "revelation" about an aspect of my personal life—which, although not a secret, was something he had heard from another person—had taken me by surprise. My current state of high emotion about what my family and I were going through had made it difficult for me to be at my analytic best with him. At the same time, I also understood—partly as a result of having recently gone through an unusually difficult personal experience—that it could not be otherwise: there was no way I could be entirely calm and thoughtful, living up to some unrealistic analytic ideal. I had done the best I could have at that point. That's life, and doing analysis is part of life. So I felt my patient and I would work with it further and, hopefully, learn more over time.

Much later that day, I also found myself thinking about his comment about my having "missed the boat", and wished I had asked him more about what that meant to him, beyond the surface colloquialism. The next day, Mr Martin began his session by saying he had met his friend Hal and his wife, Ellen, at a chamber music concert the previous evening. Ellen was the psychologist who had heard about my having a transgendered child and told her husband; he, in turn had shared it with my patient. Among other things, they had discussed this news about my family, and Ellen had become tearful.

"She said the way you, your husband, your children, your family and friends, have all dealt with your child being transgendered has been quite something. 'Moving and powerful,' that's what she called it. It makes her cry, she said, because she thinks of how her parents were up in arms because she married a Jewish man, not a Catholic one. She converted to Judaism. They still have a hard time with that, she said. They all meet each other, sure, but they're not really connected. And then here you are, all of you, you have a child whose gender is now different from the one he was born with, and she said you're all very connected. In fact, she told me your son is now engaged, and you seem to love your future daughter-in-law, too." I leaned forward a bit in my chair, my ears perking up. "You said, '*seem to*,'" I pointed out. He laughed out loud. "Okay, okay, I get it," he acknowledged. "You know what? It pisses me off, this whole everyone's-all-lovey-dovey shit. I wish there was someone who was unhappy in all of this. Seems fucking unnatural that all of you are one big happy family."

I said, "Do you imagine, perhaps, that it was all effortless, all along? That there was no conflict, no one had a hard time? That loving deeply and consistently is an easy thing to do—comes smoothly, to me and to my family? That dealing with a change like this in one's life and family would not require massive internal and external work, *and* good help from many, many people? Because if so, yes, I can understand that *that* must seem fucking unnatural. The question, though, is *what makes it necessary for you to believe that that's how it all happened—that it was all such smooth sailing?*" And then, surprisingly, I saw that Mr Martin was crying, something I had never seen him do in the analysis. In fact, he had scoffed at the idea of crying in analysis, saying he had done enough of that in his life and that he wasn't here to *cry*, he was here to *fix* things.

I asked what had made him tearful. Through his tears, he said, "I think what you're not understanding is that *I know otherwise*, which is what makes this so difficult. Ellen told me that your son had been in analysis since high school, so quite a few years now, and that you'd all got help in dealing with the transition. She said one could see how affected you and your husband were by this, and yet how clear about what you had to do to help *both* your children. I envy your kids. I really envy them having parents like you and your husband. And I hate you for not being my real mother. If that sounds crazy, I don't care."

"You're afraid I won't understand," I said.

"Yes," he replied. "I *don't* think it was easy for you. I think it must have been very difficult for you. For all of you. I'm not an idiot. I understand that. What's awful is it was hard, and *you still did it.*"

"That I was willing to do the hard work involved in loving through difference and crises—whatever—but loving and being together. That's what you missed growing up, right?"

He cried again. "Right. I think of my parents; they were so clueless." I recalled, privately, that yesterday he had felt that *I* was clueless. "And I'll tell you, there were times I felt like being a girl would have been much better for me in my family. You know, I've told you how I think my mother didn't like boys and men very much. Even Alex [his brother] she liked, *because he looked like her mother*, for heaven's sake. That home was no place for a boy to grow up in. And my snivelling father couldn't stand up for himself, let alone for me."

"That home was not a home where a boy like you felt loved and accepted," I mused, "and you wished at times you were a girl. Maybe that would have gotten you more love and attention. Makes me wonder, also—when you say that, could it be you believe my daughter turned into my son because she was not getting enough love and attention from me and my husband as a girl? Or we made it difficult for her to come into her own as a young woman?"

"I *wish!*" he exclaimed. "That would make things feel a bit better, to think your child had been through a tough time because she wasn't loved enough. But my problem is more, I think, she's been loved a lot, too much perhaps. Through thick and thin, male and female, everything."

"Today, you don't feel I missed the boat with her," I said. "What you're saying today is more that it makes you very sad that my child might have received from me, and from his father, what you didn't get from your parents. And what you would like from me, isn't it? I think that's the biggest secret here: that you want me to love you deeply, profoundly, as you are, even when you're trying your best to push me away. And that it's heartbreaking for you to think that you might be getting from me, your analyst, the attention and caring that you never got from your own parents. You want it from me, but it also makes you sad when you get it."

"Sometimes, I know I'm giving you shit, because you *do* understand, and I don't like that feeling either. Makes me feel needy and weak—" His voice trailed off. After a few moments, he spoke again. "You said this thing about the boat, not missing the boat, or missing the boat. You often ask me what it means, when I make remarks like that. You didn't yesterday, but what I was thinking about last night, after I got home from the concert, was how my mother had not come to the airport to see me off when I left Argentina. She made some silly excuse and so my father came, and some of the other family members, but not her." This was new information for me.

"How painful for you," I said. "Why do you think she did that?"

"Well, my father said not to be angry at her, it was too painful for her to say goodbye to me. Too painful for her?" His voice became louder. "Too painful for *her?* What about too fucking painful for *me?* I was only twenty-three. She couldn't come say goodbye to me at the airport? Well, fuck that, I say!"

"So much safer for you," I reflected, "to feel angry, than to know how hurt you were—and are—that she couldn't deal with her feelings enough to be there for *you*. And this, I think, is what you feel I've been able to do for my young adult child, who, as you probably know, is very close to the age you were when you left your motherland."

"I do know that," he said. "So my mother couldn't even come to the airport to say goodbye when I was leaving the country, and you've been able to somehow negotiate this whole business of saying goodbye to a daughter, and hello to the son she's become, and through all of it, to love your child. For whoever he is." His voice broke again. "I know you're right about my wanting that from you. That's what I've always wanted to have from all the women I've ever been with. And I ask you, is that too much to ask for, in one's life?"

With this poignant and beautiful question, the session drew to a close, helping us, in later months, to work more deeply and effectively with this painful, profound, and unmet longing Mr Martin had been struggling with for his entire life.

Mrs Dillon

Mrs Dillon was an elementary school teacher in her fifties when she came to me for treatment. Her internist had suggested that she enter therapy after a number of visits to the emergency room due to feeling faint and short of breath. Since all organic workups had been negative, her doctor thought that her symptoms might have been caused by anxiety. She said she was not aware of feeling anxious, but that the symptoms had begun after a new principal arrived at her school. The previous principal had been male and younger than she, and they had gotten along well. The new principal, however, was a woman, also in her fifties, and Mrs Dillon experienced her as a demanding perfectionist. When she would come to the classroom to observe, Mrs Dillon would start making errors—and when she made errors she would berate herself and feel depressed. It was as though the world had come to an end.

Mrs Dillon had been married for twenty-four years and had three grown children—two sons and a daughter—who were all unmarried professionals. She described her husband as a "very helpful man, and kind" who tolerated her rather compulsive housecleaning and need for order at all costs. She told me that this was what both her parents expected of her while she was growing up: beginning when she was a young girl, there had been chores to be done, homework to be completed, and dinner to be helped with. All six of her siblings—four sisters and two brothers—had to help. Not being able to do it all, and efficiently, was not permissible. As she grew up she could not tolerate messiness, chaos, or imperfection. In reality, her parents had both died when she was in her forties. In fantasy, however, they seemed alive and well, in her profound identifications with exactly that which she had most detested in them. And now it appeared that the demanding and perfectionist parts of her parents—and of herself—had materialised in the external form of Mrs Terrell, the new principal from hell, to cause her great anxiety.

Based on what I had heard, I outlined the various treatment routes she could take. I told her that in my opinion, if she could allow herself to be in analysis, it would give us the deepest and broadest coverage of her history and her life—and, hopefully, help her understand what was troubling her so profoundly and how it could be improved. She decided, for various reasons, that she could only come three times a week at that point, but felt comfortable using the couch, and so we began on that basis.

Mrs Dillon had been in treatment for only a few months when she walked into a session and sat down on the couch, saying, "Today I need to look at you as we talk." She went on to say that the night before, she had met an old friend from college, Linda, for dinner. Linda had gone on to medical school and become a psychiatrist, while Mrs Dillon had gone into education. They had met now after almost a year, and when Mrs Dillon shared with Linda that she was in treatment with me, Linda said she knew me slightly and thought I was very good. Then she asked, "Have you heard? Or maybe Abbasi told you yourself? Her older kid's transgendered." Mrs Dillon looked at me carefully as she spoke, and I found myself wondering what she was trying to determine.

This was about two years after the vignette reported above, and emotionally, I felt myself to be in a markedly different place; time, internal work, and external support had helped all of us move on with our lives. My son was now a psychologist, enjoyed his work, and would be getting married in a few months. My younger child, my husband, and I were past the intense mourning we had experienced during the first year or so of my son's transition. Having gone through a life-changing event, we had all, as a family, grown more deeply connected to each other, and our lives together felt even more precious than before.

At the invitation of a psychoanalytic institute on the East Coast, I had also discussed a paper on the topic of treating transgendered individuals. This had proved to be quite helpful as I thought about, and articulated, areas of both agreement and intense disagreement with the paper's author. More than that, it had been an intensely emotional experience. Through tears and laughter, I pointed out some of the subtle—and not so subtle—instances, in the work outlined by the presenter, of blaming the transgendered individual's parents, and raised questions about the validity of such assumptions. The audience raised similar challenges for the author, and long after our discussion I remained in contact with many of those present, via email and phone; we had formed an informal group, some of us following the lives of our children and others the evolving analytic literature on transgendered individuals.

I had certainly not "forgotten" the losses and pain, but seeing my son happy and settling down—and recognising the deep bonds between him, his future wife, and my younger child—was very reassuring. My husband and I were rediscovering pleasure in our life together and looking ahead. So my response to Mrs Dillon's revealing the "revelation" her friend had made to her was more one of open curiosity about her feelings.

Mrs Dillon said that she had been "shocked" to hear this news from her friend; it was hard for her to think that anything had happened in my life that was anything but "perfect". I had seemed to her, she said, "to have it all—the nice big home, your career, your writing and presenting"—she had looked me up on Google before coming to see me—"your rather exotic appearance. But you obviously don't have it all."

"What a declaration that is!" I said. "How could *anyone* have it all?"

"Well, some people do—everything neat and clean and squared away in their lives. No chaos, no confusion, no stuff spilling over."

"You seem to be describing a well-organised closet," I said—"the ones shown on TV after a room makeover by a professional organiser, rather than the mind or life of a human being."

She smiled a little and sighed, "Maybe. Maybe so." Then she looked carefully at me again. "You don't seem to be mad."

"Why would I be?" I asked.

With some diffidence, she said, "Well, I was sure you would be, that I 'found out' about this thing about your life. But maybe it's never been a secret, after all."

"You sound both relieved and disappointed," I said, "and you are looking for something in my face today, it seems to me. Am I understanding that correctly?"

She laughed in a self-conscious way, as though I had found *her* out. Then she lay down on the couch. "You're right about that," she admitted. "I wanted reassurance that you weren't angry with me as I spoke about this. And I wanted to see what else I could learn from your expressions. When Linda told me, I thought, oh, that must have been a thorn in Abbasi's side. I bet she didn't like having that in her life, and having to deal with it. You know, something different, problematic. So I guess I just wanted to be able to check your face when I told you I knew."

I said she sounded rather frightened; she was obviously worried that I'd be mad at her. The question, however, was why I would be mad at her for talking to me about an aspect of my life she had heard about that was real. So now I wondered whether the issue was not that I might be mad at her for learning the truth about this, but rather that *I might be mad at her if I knew she was feeling some satisfaction—or perhaps even pleasure—from knowing this about me.*

There was a long silence. Then she said, "It's true. I don't like to say yes to it, but it *is* true. I'm glad if you had a hard time, I'm glad everything is not perfect in your life. I mean, I'm also sorry you all went through tough stuff and all that, but really, it's all mixed up in my mind."

"All the feelings, together," I commented. "Feeling a little sorry I had to struggle, being really glad I don't have it all, and afraid I'll be mad at you for feeling this way—this satisfaction and pleasure you're getting."

Another silence, after which Mrs Dillon said, "Well, Linda asked me what I thought about how this might have affected you. And you know what, I think you must have handled it the way you seem to handle everything else. Flawlessly, perfectly. That's what I think."

"Business as usual?" I asked. "Is that what you imagine?"

"Yes! Okay, let's get this all sorted out, cleaned up, organised, and let's move on now," she said emphatically. I was struck not only by her perception of me as a cold automaton, but also by her highly unrealistic and idealised image of me taking care of—even efficiently disposing of—emotionally laden and difficult circumstances in my life.

I shared this with her, and over the next several sessions we were able to understand more about her concerns regarding her "not so nice" hurtful feelings toward me that had "spilled out" into the treatment in an untidy, chaotic way. She especially linked her image of me as an efficient automaton to how she saw her mother, and I pointed out that this was also part of herself as she expected herself to be: her idealised image of how *she* should function, and her idealised image of how she thought *I* functioned. We discussed her apparent assumption that I would find it complimentary to be told that I must handle crises in my life without batting an eye, which implied that she believed I needed to be perfect and feel perfect, *just like she did*. No wonder, I said, that she found it difficult to come for more frequent sessions: if both of us had a need to always keep things clean, how would we handle the messes that are an inevitable part of life—and which would come up during an analysis—with more clarity if we met more often?

This comment, in particular, seemed to relieve and intrigue Mrs Dillon. Her associations led to her principal and her anxiety that this woman would find her teaching somehow lacking and give her a poor evaluation. I said, "This is what you are also afraid of here, with me—that I would find you terribly lacking if you're not perfect, and wouldn't like you. You imagine I can't stand my life being imperfect. The main problem is, though, your own difficulty in tolerating your own, and others', imperfections, and seeing them as part of the stuff of life. That makes life really miserable for you, because every time, when an imperfection pops up in your functioning or your life—as it's bound to—you see it as an outrage, and a failure on your part."

During the next few months, an important focus of our work was her distaste for her sadistic feelings of wishing to hurt or humiliate me, her fear that I would be mad at her for having such feelings, and her problematic and idealised "setting the bar too high" for herself and others.

The relief she felt as we worked with this gave her hope that our work would be genuinely helpful to her, and made her feel less afraid that I could not handle "messes" in the analysis (just as her parents could not handle messy rooms or messy feelings). About three months after first discussing her friend's "revelation" of the supposed "mess" in my life (which she imagined I had cleaned up as coolly and efficiently as she used to mop up spills in her family's kitchen), Mrs Dillon asked for a fourth weekly hour, thus giving us a chance to work together in greater depth.

Discussion

We've come a long way from the unrealistic analytic ideal that the patient should know very little about the analyst's personal life, and that the patient's knowledge of events in the analyst's life would interfere with the development and analysis of the transferences. As I wrote in Chapter One, I do not agree with this in its entirety. I believe that things happen in our lives, and that patients may learn about some of them; with others, we may to decide to inform patients about them ourselves. Our job, as analysts, is to keep working with our patients in the deepest and most honest way we can, and to try to help them understand what information that has been revealed to them by others means to them and what they feel about "knowing" what they now know.

In the detailed clinical material above, two patients were informed about a significant fact of my personal life. Each brought it into their work with me, and each had different reactions and responses to what they had learned. These, in turn, led to different pathways of exploration for each. For Mr Martin, the predominant feelings evoked had to do with his longing to be loved unconditionally for himself, his envy of a child who could be loved in this way, his wanting such love from me, and his grief and rage about not having received it from his parents. With Mrs Dillon, we learned that within her unrealistic idea that I would have been able to deal with having a transgendered child without missing a beat, so to speak, was a highly problematic, malignantly idealised image of me. This led us to her idealised demands of herself and what she imagined others expected of her, which—because the bar she set for herself, and the one she believed others set for her, was unattainably high—caused her great anxiety and depression. Her wish to hurt me and her hope that revealing what she had learned would distress and embarrass me were also clear, and allowed us an inroad into her sadistic feelings, which were also a source of significant difficulty for her.

Reflecting upon special events that alter the usual analytic routine, Weiss (1975) writes:

> By the term "special events" I mean anything that alters or intrudes upon the basic analytic situation. This includes an endless list of possibilities. Let me name a few to clarify what I have in mind. It might be a telephone call, a knock at the door, a missed session

or late arrival by the analyst, a broken elevator and the patient having to walk up the stairs to the office, a loud disturbing noise in the street or next office, meeting the patient outside of the office setting, not presenting the bill to the patient at the usual time or in the usual way, etc. The list is endless. Hopefully these "special" or unforeseen events will occur very infrequently, but no analysis continues very long without some intrusion into the basic analytic situation. *There is a spectrum from the most trivial change in the analytic routine or analytic environment to the most unusual and dramatic.* (p. 69, italics added)

I agree: during every analysis, there are minor disruptions, or changes, in the frame; there are also significant events in the analyst's life. This cannot be avoided—and at least some patients, sooner or later, will hear about these events from other people. What we do with this information, and how we facilitate its exploration in the analysis for the patient's benefit, is the challenge.

Strean (1981) writes:

The extra-analytic contact is a fact of therapeutic life for many analysts and patients. It has values and potential hazards, as do other departures from routine, such as cancellations by the analyst, vacations of the analyst, *hearing realistic gossip about the analyst*, and the analyst raising his fees. The best means of utilising extra-analytic contacts constructively is by subjecting them to analytic exploration. As Greenson (1967) and other analysts have reiterated (Katz, 1978; Tarnower, 1966; Weiss, 1975), whatever the source, whether picked up in the consultation room or from an extra-analytic contact, *knowledge about the analyst is usually the vehicle for unconscious fantasy and must become the subject matter for analysis.* (p. 257, italics added)

Horowitz (1996) suggests that we work with the emergence of the patient's information about the analyst as we might work with a dream: that is, by looking at "the day residue" against which this new information, given to the patient by others, is being revealed in the analysis and by asking for associations to it. He writes:

Using minimal cues from the environment, we attempt to make the strange or unknown into the familiar. Picture again the analytic situation. The patient generally knows little about the analyst; however, little does not mean nothing. The patient has heard of the analyst, of his or her reputation, might have read something the analyst wrote, heard some gossip about the analyst, or know something of the analyst's history or family. At the very least, the analyst's voice, person, appearance, office, telephone manner all provide what in the psychology of dreaming might be termed the day residue (this is an analogy, not an exact correspondence). *There is no blank screen of the analytic circumstances.* (p. 203, italics added)

Another viewpoint is that all such information brought to the analytic session is a disruption, an attack on the setting. In this regard, Ambrosiano (2005), although not specifically discussing the issue of the patient's bringing in what she has learned about her analyst, writes:

I am thinking of what we often call attacks on the setting: bringing gifts, listening to recorded conversations with external people in the setting, asking the analyst to read letters, questioning the rules of payment and times, bringing exciting gossip about the analyst's colleagues to the session, right up to promiscuous and bizarre behaviour that aims, in phantasy, to embarrass the analyst regarding his professional world. (p. 1622)

On my part, I do not view what Ambrosiano calls attacks on the settings as attacks. Instead, I view all of the above as the patient's way of communicating something that, at that point in the analysis, cannot be communicated, by the patient, in any other way.

Many analysts work with the attitude that what our patients learn about us, and inform us of, can be useful in exploring and understanding their inner conflicts and in deepening—rather than curtailing—the transference, *provided the analyst is open to this possibility.* In this regard, Appelbaum and Diamond (1993) write:

We are all familiar with the astonishing lengths to which patients will go in order not to know us—or not to know that they know. Analysts may be more than willing to relax behind the pseudoanonymity created by their implicit agreement with patients that the analyst's personal life is forbidden territory. Polite patients generally enter into this agreement immediately, when an "ordinary" question such as "Were you away for the weekend?" does not evoke the ordinary response, but rather silence, or a counter-question. Although the analyst's asking what the patient had in mind is intended as an invitation to free associate, it is usually understood first as a reminder that wanting to know about the analyst is "wrong." (p. 146)

Crastnopol (1997) writes in a similar vein:

> I would like to restate that depending on the patient's own internal makeup, accidents of the analyst's witting or unwitting self-revelation, and tricks of fate, the patient may discover and seek to interpret any aspect of the analyst's personality or private life. The patient's expressed or silent reaction to experiencing more of the analyst as a person may markedly influence his or her internal use of the analyst and of the analytic encounter—for good, for ill, and for both. *This effect will be haphazard unless the analyst accepts his or her extratherapeutic identity as a meaningful part of their mutual analytic scrutiny.* (p. 278, italics added)

Phillips (1998) describes clinical material from his work with a male heterosexual who discovered, during the course of his analysis, that his analyst was homosexual. The patient learned this by first checking details available to him—where the analyst currently lived and whether he lived alone or with a spouse. Later he heard from another person, more directly, that the analyst was homosexual. Phillips's paper provides a rare window into the richness and depth that can become part of the analytic discourse that arises when patients learn, from others, about important aspects of the analyst's life and bring this into their treatment. Phillips raises important questions when he talks about "the example of one analyst who feared that a heterosexual patient might unknowingly enter analysis with a homosexual analyst. Should the patient learn later on of the analyst's sexual orientation, was the concern, the patient might suffer a malignant paranoid regression" (p. 1195). He adds:

> Initially I was puzzled by the analyst's apprehension. How would this situation differ, I wondered, from an analysand's learning of

the analyst's marriage or divorce, the birth of a child, the illness or death of a family member, or a religious or political affiliation— all of them events, beliefs, or attitudes, revealing and personal, that can find their way into the public domain? And what of the analyst who becomes pregnant during an analysis unbeknownst to the patient? The analyst's pregnancy, like the analyst's sexual orientation, can resonate with the patient's most deep-seated wishes and fears. The related issue of what shows and what is hidden about one's analyst is also relevant to both. Further, the discovery of either would obviously affect each analysand differently and unpredictably. However unsettling such news is for the patient, the analytic stance is to explore the depth and breadth of such reactions, including the accompanying affective experience, their function as resistance, their transference meanings, and so on. (Ibid. p. 1196)

Phillips presents us with an excellent reminder of a basic analytic goal: that all the patient brings to us is a gift of communication, whatever the form. If the form is destructive to the patient or to others (e.g., suicidality, physical assault, or other forms of destructiveness towards others), I focus first on ensuring that my patient, and others, are safe; then I work with my patient to understand the meanings of her dangerous behaviours. If, however, the form of communication my patient has adopted is not particularly dangerous—but is unusual or jarring for me and makes me anxious—I work on trying to understand my own reactions so that I can better tolerate what the patient is doing to, and with, me. In the greater space created by genuine tolerance of a different form of "free association", rich and effective analytic work can be done.

In the following chapter, I present an example of an unusual form of communication and the complex understanding of it that my patient and I developed over the course of our work.

PART III

WHEN MACHINES INTRUDE UPON CLINICAL SPACE

CHAPTER FOUR

A patient's tape recording of analytic sessions

Introduction

Historically, psychoanalysts have claimed that they could best treat patients who communicate by saying whatever comes to mind—the fundamental rule of psychoanalysis. The patient who insisted on action in an analytic treatment was seen as not quite suitable for such treatment and given a poor prognosis. While it is true that certain actions cause great disruption in an analytic treatment (e.g., addictive behaviours, self-mutilation, violence toward others, and suicidality, to name a few), I find that there is hardly any patient who does not communicate via action in one form or another—and that an analyst has to be able to pay attention to, and be interested in, action and actions, both big and small, for this mode of communication to be treated as a source of important information. Child analysts, who accept the usefulness—indeed the *requirement*—of the child's actions and play as the method for transmission of information in the analytic setting, have much less difficulty, even in adult analysis, with action. Adult analysts have struggled much more with this notion. This chapter addresses the issue of action in analysis and the value of creating an analytic space that houses not only the words our (adult) patients use to express their innermost worlds, but also the actions.

I illustrate this idea by presenting detailed clinical material from the treatment of a woman who tape-recorded, for two and a half years, each and every analytic session she had with me. This was accepted in the analysis as something my patient felt she needed to do, even as she talked to me about it. As we worked together to understand the feelings, conflicts, and memories connected to her complex behaviour, the patient gradually felt less and less need for the action and ultimately stopped altogether. The analysis then continued, progressed well, and a planned termination took place after ten years of analytic work.

Clinical material

Mrs Green

It was a cold fall day. I was sitting in my office looking at Mrs Green as she sat in a chair a little distance from mine. The light from the shaded lamp behind her highlighted her brown hair as it curled softly around her face, the premature wrinkles I had noticed at our first meeting a little less pronounced today in the muted light. She sat erect, her clasped hands resting in her lap. On a little table by her side was a handbag: plain, gray, and sensible-looking. We were meeting for the third time. She had been referred to me by a psychiatrist who had treated her with antidepressants and once-a-week psychotherapy for two years. He was now moving to a hospital where he would be doing only inpatient work, and had suggested that she contact me for ongoing treatment.

Mrs Green had just finished telling me how unhappy she was in her marriage. She had started discussing this with her previous therapist and was more and more aware of her unhappiness in living with her husband. She added that this was one of the reasons she felt she needed to continue in therapy. She paused and looked around the room. After a few moments she said, "I should tell you at this point that while I was seeing Dr Hassan [her previous therapist], I started to tape record my therapy sessions with him." She opened her handbag and took out a mini-cassette recorder. "Would it would be all right if I continue to do the same here with you?"

I sat back, taken completely by surprise. In everything I had ever read about therapy and psychoanalysis, this dilemma had never been addressed. I heard imaginary voices of instructors and supervisors emphasising the need for reflection in treatment rather than action, and realised that these denoted my own anxiety about what my patient had just asked me. I was a candidate in psychoanalytic training at that point, and it felt critically important that I follow what I perceived as "analytic ideals"—which, of course, were a mixture of what I had seen, heard, read, and believed was the way an analyst should behave. Rather hesitantly, I said, "I understand you feel a need to use a tape recorder during your sessions. There is obviously a history to this that I do not yet know, but I think it'll be helpful for us to talk about what this might mean. Hopefully, we'll learn a great deal from doing that." Mrs Green looked at me, her face quite expressionless, and put the recorder in her handbag as the session drew to a close.

In our next meeting we spoke about how to proceed in terms of our future work together and decided to start with twice-a-week psychotherapy, with the idea of increasing the sessions in the near future. At that time, I believed that it would help her to be seen in intensive psychotherapy, but I had not consciously thought of my work with her as a possible psychoanalytic treatment. It is only in looking back that I can recognise that my inability to visualise her in psychoanalysis had to do with my own limited experience as an analyst, as well as concerns about her need to record the sessions. Necessary as it might have been for *her*, I experienced it initially as a need, on her part, to *act on* certain feelings rather than talk about them, and felt this did not bode well for a psychoanalytic treatment, with its framework of free association, self-reflection, delayed gratification, and the ability to tolerate a certain level of frustration.

A few sessions after she began treatment, Mrs Green came in one day, sat down, placed her handbag squarely in her lap, took her tape recorder from it, removed the handbag, and proceeded to place the tape recorder on my desk close to where I was sitting. She then said to me "I have to tell you that I have been thinking about what you said earlier in terms of this tape recorder. I know that we need to understand what it means, and that that would be the most important thing to do here; however, I feel that even as we try to understand what it means, I *have* to use this to record the sessions." As I sat back in my chair, feeling bewildered by her insistence and confused about how to proceed, I found myself thinking of a conversation between Alice and the Cheshire Cat:

"Would you tell me, please, which way I ought to go from here?"
"That depends a good deal on where you want to get to," said the Cat.
"I don't much care where—" said Alice.
"Then it doesn't matter which way you go," said the Cat.
"—so long as I get *somewhere*," Alice added as an explanation.
"Oh, you're sure to do that," said the Cat, "if you only walk long enough."

Lewis Carroll, *Alice's Adventures in Wonderland*

Mrs Green used the tape recorder to record her therapy and her analytic sessions with me over a period of two and a half years. There were many times, especially at first, when I felt anxious and constrained by the presence of the tape recorder. At times I found myself holding back from saying something, thinking, "This is being recorded." I worried about what she would ultimately do with the tapes, and whether they would come back one day to haunt me in some form. While she was in psychotherapy, she would place the tape recorder on the desk close to her. Later, when she started psychoanalytic treatment, she placed the tape recorder on a small table near the couch, on which I kept a box of tissues and a few other items. I was aware that she had saved all of the tapes she had recorded with her previous therapist and that they were in a suitcase in her home. She told me she was labelling tapes of our work together and collecting them in a bag.

I felt like Alice, who was confused and uncertain about where she was going—but I also felt like the Cat, who reassured her that she was sure to get *somewhere* if she only walked long enough. I did not yet know what the destination would be. I sensed that her use of the tape recorder and our work to understand the meanings of this behaviour, even as she recorded her sessions with me, had aspects of an acting out on her part and a joint enactment by both of us. More importantly, however, it was a vehicle that allowed her to gradually communicate certain feelings, needs, wishes, and memories in her treatment. Her reasons for using the tape recorder were as obscure to her initially as they were to me. As we worked together to analyse material that surfaced over time, however, much was understood about what this behaviour on her part represented. We eventually understood that her use of the tape recorder and the recorded tapes encompassed multiple areas of feeling and memory that were painful, anxiety-provoking, and frightening. It was only later that all of these could be articulated in the analysis. My work with Mrs Green allowed me to experience firsthand the usefulness of inviting in a patient's communications in whatever form he or she is able to bring them to my analytic door. I also learned over time to consider each communication as a guide to a part of the mind in which the patient cannot yet fully recall, feel, or articulate—and, in some instances, an aspect of the mind that has yet to be formed (Levine, Reed, & Scarfone, 2013).

The patient's background

Mrs Green was in her early forties when she first came to see me. A former schoolteacher, she described growing up as the youngest in a sibship of four with an older brother and two older sisters. Her father was a supervisor in a factory and her mother a homemaker. She described her mother as being extremely emotionally distant from her all during her childhood and adult life. Her mother had been an excellent housekeeper, but Mrs Green never felt that she and her mother connected in any meaningful way. She described memories of feeling terribly bored and lonely in childhood, attempting to talk with her mother about it, and being rebuffed. She remembered feeling that she was asking her mother for too much and that she was a burden to her. She recalled her father with a great deal of warmth, describing him as a jovial man who loved to sing and dance at parties.

When she was eighteen, her father died of a heart attack. In her early twenties, she established and maintained a couple of relationships with men. She was especially fond of one of them, but he ultimately broke off the relationship for reasons she claimed were unclear to her. Soon after this she met and subsequently married her husband, charmed by his good looks and his happy-go-lucky demeanour. "Only later," she said, "did I realise that he was very controlling, careless with money, and often cruel to our children." When Mrs Green was in her thirties, her mother died of cancer.

She had five children during her marriage, three boys and two girls. One of her sons, John, died of a terminal illness, at the age of twenty. It was after his death that she had started therapy with Dr Hassan.

The beginning of treatment

Within six months of starting treatment with me, Mrs Green increased the frequency of her sessions from two to four times a week. During this time, she was essentially dealing with her feelings about the loss of her previous therapist, the death of her son, and severe unhappiness in her marriage. As a result of this early work, and as her relationship with me deepened, she started thinking more actively about leaving her husband. She had been thinking about this, she said, for a long time, but had never felt able to do it. After some discussion with her children, she informed her husband of her decision and moved into an apartment of her own. This brought into the treatment her loneliness, her anxiety about finances and health insurance, and her husband's anger at her. Mrs Green's commitment to treatment deepened, and her involvement with me was clearly stronger at this point.

During her first year of treatment I would from time to time bring up her use of the tape recorder and, with her, wonder about it. Her associations to my questions usually were that between sessions it helped her to be able to replay them. It appeared at this point that the use of the tape recorder served a supportive function for her when she was alone, and was a way of keeping me with her when we were separated. Around this time, having worked with Mrs Green in intensive treatment for about a year, I had grown to appreciate that she had the capacity for reflection and introspection and realised that there was no reason we should not work together in a full psychoanalytic treatment. I was considering starting another analytic case at this point, and although still a candidate in analytic training, I was fortunate to find a supervisor who listened with serious consideration to my presentation of the case material and agreed that the patient's recording of the sessions, although interesting, curious, and obviously worth understanding, was in no way an indication that she should not be in a psychoanalytic treatment (it should be noted that other supervisors I consulted with felt that Mrs Green's urgent need to record her analytic sessions was an indication of poor affect tolerance, impulsivity, and need for action rather than reflection and verbalisation and counselled me to not take her on as an analytic control case). A few months after the end of our first year of work, Mrs Green started five-times-a-week psychoanalysis on the couch.

The multiple meanings of Mrs Green's use of her tape recorder

1. As a transitional object

   Mrs Green's transition from the sitting position to using the couch was marked by many associations related to not being able to see me. This brought to her mind thoughts about her son's death and not being able to see her previous therapist any longer; she felt that being on the couch was like losing me. I noticed around this time that before lying down every day, she would remove her shoes and, toward the end of the session, take time to slowly lace up her shoes, while making remarks about the weather, as though we were having a leisurely chat. Also, she would frequently pause at the door at the end of the hour to ask me a question. I asked whether she was aware of this and what she thought about it. She noted that doing what she did allowed her to stay with me a little longer. I said, "It's important for you to feel that we are together and I am here for you. As you lace up your shoes and ask me questions at the end of the session, it allows you to have a little bit more of me." Could it be, I asked, that an aspect of recording my voice on tape and being able to listen to it when I was not there served the same purpose: having me with her when I was not there, and having more of me than she would have if we were together for only forty-five minutes?

   She reflected that she *did* find it helpful. It was soothing for her to be able to hear my voice between sessions, particularly on weekends when we didn't meet. The brief separations reminded her of times in her childhood when she would turn to her mother, feeling terribly distressed, and her mother would make unhelpful comments, indicating that she should try to deal with her feelings herself. I said, "It sounds as though being able to turn on my tape-recorded voice when we are not together makes you feel that perhaps I'm *not* like your mother, who was not available to you when you were distressed and lonely." She remembered that often during her treatment with Dr Hassan, she had asked him if he could see her more than once a week. He always said he thought it would be helpful, but he never offered to make concrete arrangements to do so. After asking him this question several times she had started to feel that perhaps she was "asking for too much", and that despite his polite affirmative response every time, he really did not want to see her more often. At that time, listening to recorded sessions between the actual sessions had clearly been a way of having more of him than she felt he had been willing to give her. "It must also have created a feeling of togetherness," I said, "when you were in fact separate." In this way, the tape recorder seemed to serve the purpose of a transitional object (Winnicott, 1953) for Mrs Green.

2. As an aid in the avoidance of problematic feelings
    About a year and a half into the treatment, Mrs Green started to observe difficulty in feeling angry with people, including with me. She said that at times she had left a session feeling upset over something I had said. She would then go home and listen to the tape recording and would be relieved to hear on the tape that I had not, in fact, actually said what she thought I had said. She would then stop feeling angry. I replied, "Sounds like you are using the tapes to quickly defuse your feelings of anger toward me, as if the tapes are a neutral third party in the room and you can check with them to determine whether I *really* said something about which you *should* be offended."

    I wondered what would be dangerous about going with the feeling of anger and telling me about it when she felt it. Her associations to this included her fears that I would not then consider her a good patient. She spoke about her mother's inability to tolerate any feelings of irritability, sadness, or anger on her part. In a similar vein, she added that there were times when she felt I had said something to her that was tender, which made her feel happy, but it was hard for her to tell me about that in the session. Instead, she would replay the tape of that session later and would feel soothed and comforted by once more hearing my voice saying something tender to her. I observed, "It's obviously difficult for you to tell me both about feeling touched by me and about feeling very angry at me—but maybe the greater difficulty is even telling *yourself* about such feelings." Both feelings were dangerous, but what was not yet clear, I said, was what was so frightening about these feelings that they had to be dealt with in this way.

3. As a vehicle for the expression of hostility

Close to the end of the second year of her treatment, sometime before my summer break, Mrs Green began to have feelings of tremendous depression and thoughts of suicide. I tried to understand the reason for the emergence of these feelings at this point. She seemed very depressed during the session, and her thoughts about wishing to be dead strengthened as the days passed. She began to talk about killing herself on the anniversary of the death of her son, stating that in this way she would "not be hurting her family too much", because that particular day was "already a rotten time for them". I asked "Do you really believe that your children would not be affected by your suicide simply because it would occur on the day that already marks the death anniversary of your son?" After a pause she acknowledged that she did know that that was not completely correct, but it had *felt* correct to her because of how she had been feeling for the past few weeks.

Referring to my upcoming summer break, I again pointed out the context in which her feelings of depression and thoughts of killing herself were emerging. I recalled with her another episode of severely depressed feelings she had had several months earlier, when I had gone away for my winter break. She now began to talk about her anger at her son "for dying and leaving me alone to deal with it", which became connected to her father's death and her mother's una-vailability to her all of her life. I said, "It's all connected, isn't it, your feeling very angry at people and feeling suicidal?" She said she felt very guilty about her son, who had died so young. His father had at times physically abused him during his early years, and she wished she could have spared him that ordeal. She wondered if she and her husband had done all they could have during their son's terminal illness. I said that I could see how she suffered from these doubts. She said that sometimes the idea of killing herself on the anniver-sary of her son's death seemed connected to atoning for his death. I could sense her tremendous conflicts about her feelings of anger and guilt and the way she was attempting to deal with them through her thoughts of suicide.

As I discussed all of this with my supervisor, he asked me if I was worried that my patient might kill herself. I said no, I was not. I felt she was having suicidal thoughts, but would not act on them. He asked how I knew that. He also asked whether I had asked her how she thought she might kill herself—a basic question even first-year psychiatry residents know to ask. I realised I had not. My supervisor then asked whether I was reflecting upon this difficult and somewhat frightening patient, and my feelings about her, in my analysis. I said no, not really, it "hadn't come up there". Whereupon my supervisor gently but firmly told me he thought I was having significant problems recognising and addressing my patient's intense rage toward me; her wish to upset me, make me worry about her, and frighten me; and her fantasy that she might destroy the progress of my analytic education by killing herself—the ultimate revenge. He said he was concerned that I had not brought these complicated interactions into my analysis and thus not allowed myself to receive much-needed help in this matter.

At that point, I had just applied for my next analytic control case. My supervisor shared with me that given the difficulty I was having with this patient, he could not support my taking on another analytic patient just yet and suggested I wait another six months. I was devastated, outraged that my progress as an analytic candidate was being derailed by this "trivial" matter—until I began discussing my work with Mrs Green in my analysis. My analyst was surprised to learn that so much had been going on in my work with her, and meanwhile I had been nonchalantly focusing only on other matters in my analysis, as though the serious issues she and I were struggling with were no big deal. He wondered whether he could interest me in looking at the way I had compartmentalised all these areas of my life and mind: my work with my patient, my supervisor's concerns, my analysis. And what did all of this have to do with my earlier life and my feelings about him?

It was only then that, very gradually, I began to recognise how Mrs Green's depression and suicidal threats were stirring up old childhood conflicts in me, which I was dealing with by minimising the seriousness of what she was struggling with. I also felt angry at her—and guilty about feeling angry—and was, therefore, not addressing her suicidality more usefully and openly with her— a suicidality that, if it led to action, could have serious repercussions not only for her, but for me. In addition, it would have indirect but powerful repercussions for my supervisor and my analyst.

I could now speak with her more openly about her suicidal feelings, and, with some trepidation (as though asking about her plans would make her more suicidal, even though I knew that the converse was true), I asked how she envisioned killing herself. She revealed that she had had thoughts of either shooting herself, putting her head in the oven with the gas on, or taking an overdose. The method did not feel meaningful to her, she said; it was the idea of being dead that seemed important. She then added, however—in a tone so calm it was chilling—that she visualised all her children, and her husband, collected around her body at the funeral, feeling dreadful about the many ways in which they had not helped or been available to her. She went on to say that she felt quite sure her husband would try to sue me if she committed suicide, because he was already very angry at me. He felt she had left him because of her work with me, and a few times he had in fact threatened to kill me—and I knew, did I not, that he owned a pistol? Now I felt the full blast of her superficially contained rage. *And it dawned on me that she wished to frighten and hurt me just as I wished to do to my supervisor and my analyst.*

I felt I could now begin to understand Mrs Green better. I brought up the cool, detached manner in which she spoke about her hope that her family would feel guilty and "dreadful" when they saw her dead body after her suicide. I noted the calm and friendly manner in which she revealed her husband's death threat to me and reminded me that he owned a firearm. And I asked whether it was perhaps easier to talk about *his* anger toward me than about *her* anger toward me when she experienced me as an unavailable and abandoning mother? She said I didn't have to worry about getting into any kind of trouble if she committed suicide. She would make sure the tapes of our work together were left in an easily visible spot, so that after she killed herself they could be heard by others and would help to protect me from lawsuits or being charged with negligence. The tapes, she said, would be "proof that you tried your best to help me".

A shiver of apprehension ran through me, and I realised it was apprehension not only about what she wanted to do to me, but also about my mounting anger at her. In a tense voice, trying to control my fear and my anger, I said, "It's a curious way you have of trying to help me. First you will kill yourself while you're in analysis with me, and then you want to try to rescue me from the possibility of your family suing me by having these tapes available as proof that I *did* try to help you. With friends like you I don't need enemies, do I?"

Mrs Green responded to this confrontation with the first signs of an emotionally laden recognition of the tremendous hostility behind her apparently concerned and helpful attitude. She said she was shocked by her wish to hurt me when I had been trying to help her—and yet, I said, the sense of shock suggested that she wanted to believe her wish to hurt me was something foreign that had over-taken her. It was difficult for her to accept that these feelings were a part of her. This discussion, which was now based on my own recog-nition of hostile and destructive wishes in the face of thwarted long-ings for my early caretakers, helped Mrs Green get in touch with the ambivalence she felt for me: her love for me *and* her wish to destroy me. Recording the sessions and preserving the tapes were intrinsic parts of a fantasy she had about wanting to hurt me—and to salve her guilt about these destructive feelings by attempting to save me, after her suicide, by leaving the tapes of our work together.[1]

4. The "father goose" fantasy and the fear of "extinction"
    When I returned from my summer break that year, Mrs Green spoke about having missed me tremendously. She described a recent tel-evision show she had seen, about William Lishman, who had been nicknamed "father goose" for his efforts to save one endangered species of geese from becoming extinct. He worked with the gos-lings immediately after they hatched, encouraging them to follow him and becoming their caretaker. As he walked and they followed him, he played a recording of the sound his ultralight glider made. The glider was shaped like a goose, and when winter arrived he planned to fly it south, followed by the goslings, so they would not die in the cold weather. The goslings, which were attached to father goose, became used to the tape-recorded sound of the glider; when winter came and he flew south, they did indeed follow him. In this way, he managed to save a small number of geese from becoming extinct. She noted with bitterness and extreme sadness that this man had spent hours and hours on their behalf, and added, "I wasn't given even half of this [much] attention by my own mother." I said that it was this sadness and the accompanying rage that she also felt in her relationship with me: "These were the feelings you were trying to tell me about," I said, "as I was leaving you to go for my summer break, through your thoughts of committing suicide."

    Mrs Green said it made her angry that there was no one who spent hours and hours with *her*, saving her from her wish to die—from becoming extinct. I said it angered her that I, unlike Father Goose, gave her only forty-five minutes five times a week. Nor did I offer to record something that would help her; *she* had to record *my* sound and carry it with her. Could it be that it was easier for her to talk about *her* plans to save *me* than about her desire for *me* to save *her*? She said, "I feel that if you don't save me I'll become extinct, like the geese. I'll cease to exist. It reminds me of the story of the velveteen rabbit." She began to talk about the story, in which a stuffed rabbit comes to life only after it is "really" loved by a little boy; without such love, the rabbit could not have existed in live form.

I said, "And that's what you feel with me—that it is only through my love in the analysis that you can 'really' come to life." She cried, and said, "Through your wanting me, really wanting me and wanting to be with me." She then told me about a memory of being six or seven, sitting with her mother in the yard one day, and her mother telling her, "I never really wanted you; you weren't planned." Mrs Green continued to cry profusely as she recalled this, wondering why her mother had told her that, feeling that her mother must have wanted to hurt her. She said she had also heard that after she was born, when her mother took her out into the yard one day, a neighbour was surprised to see her mother with a baby. To the patient this meant that her mother must not have told her neighbours that she was pregnant. She said, "It was as if all the months I was in her body, I did not exist."

This was a terrifying and painful memory for her, of feeling completely unwanted, as though her mother had wanted to make her extinct. We could begin now to understand more about her feeling that when we were not together, it was as though she did not exist—as though she had become extinct; it seemed impossible that two people could remain deeply connected and alive for each other even when they were not physically together. Hence the need for a tape recording of our time together—concrete evidence that neither of us had become extinct for the other or that we had actually killed each other off.

5. As an enactment of a childhood event

    A little more than two years after Mrs Green started seeing me, I informed her that I would be moving my office in a couple of months. The move would be to a location at a somewhat greater distance from her home. She had a profound reaction to this. She was upset because it would mean additional travel time for her, but also because she felt I was moving "to the elite side of town", and had fantasies that I would be interested only in wealthy patients who drove to my office in Jaguars. There was a powerful fear that I was getting ready to get rid of her; she felt that it was "the beginning of the end". I acknowledged the fact that she would have to drive an extra fifteen or twenty minutes to see me. I wondered, however, whether she was feeling something more about my move that we needed to examine. For the next several weeks she spoke about how distressed she was over the impending change, but said she did not think it had to do with anything other than what she had already told me.[2]

After she started seeing me in my new office, I continued to point out that her reaction, though partly based on reality, seemed to indicate some intense personal feelings, the origins of which were unclear to both of us. As I was telling her this one day, she said, "I *am* beginning to wonder whether this has to do with other things in my life." She reflected that she could remember no important changes in her life in terms of the location of her home. Then she haltingly noted that only one change came to her mind. It did not have to do with a move to another home, but rather with the fact that when she was about eleven, her father had changed his work schedule. Previously, he had worked the day shift and would come home around four in the afternoon, which meant he was available to her during the late afternoon and evening. She remembered his presence as extremely comforting, since she felt so disconnected from her mother most of the time.

Now, however, he announced that he no longer liked the day shift because of various problems at work, and he had decided to move to the afternoon shift. He then started work at three p.m. and did not return home until almost midnight. Most of the time, therefore, she did not see him at all unless her mother allowed her to stay up late. Now, amid a storm of tears, she recalled how abandoned and lonely she had felt. Her father, she said, had been like a mother to her, and when he was gone it was as if she had no mother. I said, "Your father was a father goose for you, a man who mothered you in a way in that your own mother did not." My changing the location of my office seemed to have stirred up painful feelings from the distant past related to the mothering father who had abandoned her, as she experienced it, in favour of his own well being. She seemed to feel that I, too, wanted to leave her behind—to abandon her for my own convenience in this move to a new office.

At this point, Mrs Green told me that prior to her father's change in work hours, he would often listen to the radio in the late evening. He was fond of changing stations, moving from one to the other and listening to the news. When she was young she often would sit on his knee while he was doing this. At times she felt irritated with him because he was so focused on the radio. One night she protested, asking why he wanted to listen to the same news on all the stations. "Why aren't you talking to *me*?" she demanded. Annoyed with her, he sent her to her room. I said, "You felt the radio came between you and your father." She said yes, that sometimes she had hated that radio. I now felt a similar resonance of feeling in myself about her tape recorder: I realised that at many points in our work together, I felt relegated to one side by the tape recorder and highly irritated by its presence. She seemed, to me, to be talking to the recorder rather than to me. There were also times when I resented her playing with the tape recorder as she adjusted it at the beginning of the sessions to make sure that she had pushed the correct buttons and the volume was just the way she wanted it.

I now said to her, "I'm wondering if another aspect of your using this tape recorder with me has to do with your playing out with me these interactions with your father that you are now telling me about, when you felt extremely excluded and hurt by his interest in the radio." It was as though she had been behaving with me as if she were her father and I her childhood self, so that she was with me physically but kept me subordinate to the tape recorder, just as she had felt with *her* father and *his* radio. Haltingly, she mused, "It seemed with my father that if I came between him and his radio, I would be sent to my room. If I wanted to be with him, I had to tolerate his fondness for his radio." I responded, "And in our work together you made it so that you and I could be together only if I agreed to your having a tape recorder with you."

On the day following the above session, Mrs Green arrived thirty minutes late for her session, which was extremely unusual for her. She lay down on the couch and talked about having felt confused about what time the session was to start. I noticed her vigorously rubbing her eyes every few moments. At some point during the brief time we had together that day, I commented on this and wondered what it was about. She suddenly sat up on the couch and, pointing to her eyes, said there was some irritation and redness around her eyes. She planned to see a physician about it. I wondered with her about the unusual circumstances surrounding the brief session that day: first her lateness, and now her sitting up to show me something. She said, "I don't know what's going on. I know I kept you waiting today and suddenly just now I had the feeling I had to *show* you what was wrong with my eyes."

I said, "I'm thinking also about yesterday. We had been talking about your waiting for your father to come home—the father who was both mother and father to you. Today, by forgetting the time of the session, you created a situation in which *I* had to wait for *you*, just as you used to wait for your father." I then pointed out that *she had not turned on her tape recorder that day*. She said, "Yes, I know. Somehow it doesn't seem important to do that today." I felt that she was suggesting an interesting and significant possibility: could it be that using the tape recorder during our more than two years together had been an effort on her part to *show* both of us something that she felt she could not yet begin to remember and talk about more clearly? She replied, "As though I've been using the tape recorder to tell you things I hadn't *really* forgotten but couldn't *really* remember— or maybe just couldn't talk about—but needed to show you? Yes, it does feel like that now—that I've been trying to tell you something in this way."

Over the next few days, Mrs Green used the tape recorder during some sessions but not others. She began to talk more clearly about feeling conflicted about using it. She noted that during our early work together, she would replay the tape of each session on the day of the session; however, during the past few months she had not listened to most of the tapes she had recorded. She said, "It's obviously not a question of keeping things in memory anymore. It just seems like I don't feel sure that we could be together, you and I, just the two of us."

I asked what she thought that was about. She then recalled that during her marriage her husband often accused her of distorting facts, denying that he had said something she had heard him say, or insisting that she had not told him something when she knew she had. At a certain point in her marriage, she began keeping notes of important issues they had discussed "so I could prove to him later what had really transpired." I noted the distrust and fear involved in this, and added, "You seem to feel that if there are differences in how we remember things that happened here, we could not try to understand them together. It doesn't yet feel safe to be with me without the tape recorder as a kind of witness in the room." She responded, "It just seems there would be something frightening about depending on you totally." After a pause she added, "I think that reminds me also of the way I used to feel with my mother." I said, "You feel a need to protect yourself and to protect me from some dangers that feel very real to you by continuing to use the recorder." She answered, "It really feels right now that it has something to do with what it would feel like to be just two people, you and I, in this room without the recorder. There is something good about that thought, but something frightening, too."

On the day after this, *about two and a half years into our work together*, Mrs Green stopped using the tape recorder completely. In that session and those that followed, many thoughts surfaced about her father's death. Her memories of him seemed at this time closely related to missing him as a maternal figure. Issues related to mourning his death, which I felt had previously come up in only a muted way in the analysis, now surged forth against a background of these memories. This was accompanied by intense feelings of loving me and wanting me to love her. It was as though a storm that had been held at bay now erupted in full force with all its vibrant colours and surging power. Then one day she recalled a teenaged memory of her mother. Her mother had been sitting on the couch in the living room and Mrs Green had moved over and put her head in her mother's lap. This memory—the only one she could recall of such physical closeness—was recalled with poignant and bittersweet sadness. It was accompanied in the analysis with thoughts of wanting to bring me a gift, and a few days later she brought me a brightly coloured pillow, the shades of which she felt represented the colours of my office.

I had a strange response. I could appreciate and understand that her emerging feelings for me represented progress for her and were a result of the good work we were doing together. At the same time, I found myself experiencing a need to withdraw and wanting to return the pillow to her. I decided to wait while I attempted to understand my own feelings and to work with hers. In talking about the gift, she felt she wanted to show her appreciation of me. She had noted that I sometimes used a pillow for my back in the chair I used when I sat behind the couch. I asked what her thoughts were about what I might do with the pillow. She said it was almost as though that did not matter: what was important was she should be able to give it to me and I should be able to keep it even if I did not really use it. Then, rather hesitantly, she revealed that she had had an image of the pillow in my lap and her head resting against it.

I was now able to recognise that the feelings from which I had recoiled, and with which I had felt uncomfortable, had to do with my own awareness of her intense need to be my daughter, to feel loved by me, and to be in my lap, burrowing into me. As I better understood my own conflicts about what such a need in her stirred up in me, I was able to talk with her about the painful longings she had experienced with her mother and her intense wish at this point not just to be held by me, but perhaps even to become a part of me. She said, "Yes, it seems so silly but I have had thoughts recently that I wanted to curl up like a baby and go back into you, just as a child might with a real mother." I said I did not think it was a coincidence that these intense feelings, both of missing her mothering father, and of longing for her mother—along with the feelings she was having about me—had come up at this point in the analysis, soon after she had stopped using the tape recorder. The powerful emergence of these feelings seemed related to a sense on her part that she could tolerate and begin to talk about what she was feeling in words rather than through use of the tape recorder.

Discussion

Psychoanalytic literature is replete with papers on the concepts of action, acting out, and enactments. In introducing the term "acting out", Akhtar (2009b) writes:

> This English language psychoanalytic term has been derived from the German *agieren*, "to act," which Sigmund Freud (1905e) used in describing certain aspects of the case of Dora. "Thus, she acted out an essential part of her recollections and fantasies instead of

producing it in the treatment" (p. 119). Acting out was thus seen as a resistance to remembering and free association. In the later [...] paper, "Remembering, repeating, and working through" (1914g), Freud extended the meaning of the term by including the possibility that besides serving as a resistance, acting out could also be a way of remembering. (p. 2)

Following Freud's writings on the subject, a number of early papers show analysts struggling to clarify their thinking about patients' actions in analysis. These include papers by Beres (1973), Bird (1957), Carroll (1954), Ekstein and Friedman (1950), Fenichel (1954), Anna Freud (1968), Gaddini (1982), Greenacre (1950), Kanzer (1957), Kestenberg (1968), Kucera (1968), Segel (1969), and Stein (1973), as well as many others. These papers, written in the 1950s and 1960s, elaborate on Freud's original struggles to delineate the concept of acting out and use the authors' own clinical experiences to further clarify it. Numerous later papers, such as those by Chasseguet-Smirgel (1990), Busch (1989, 2009), and Chused (1991), contributed additional perspectives to the literature.

My patient's insistence on recording her sessions with me could certainly be described as an *acting out*, about which Roughton (1993) had this to say:

The issue that defines acting out is the relation of the behaviour to the analytic process and especially to the transference relationship. The defining criterion for acting out is not the nature of the behaviour itself, nor the gravity of the behaviour, nor whether it occurs within or outside the analytic setting. Acting out may interfere with, or it may advance, the analytic process. It may serve as a resistance to remembering and communicating, or it may be a way of remembering and communicating. (p. 444)

Roughton adds:

Enactment, as a general term, means simply putting into behaviour that which one is experiencing internally [...] Boesky (Panel, 1992) regards enactments as behaviours, initiated by either analysand or analyst, that have an actualising intention. (Ibid. pp. 457–458).

Roughton then explains the concept of actualising:

> Actualisation of the transference occurs when the analysand expe-
> riences the analyst's behaviour or attitude as having fulfilled his
> wishes or expectations, often without awareness of the wish or the
> process. This would include gratifications inherent in the analytic
> process itself ... These inherent process functions may also fulfil
> specific transference fantasies for certain analysands. (Ibid. p. 458)

Different analysts have different degrees of tolerance for action on the
part of patients, and each analyst has a different tolerance for different
kinds of actions. All action, however—if it can ultimately be viewed
through the analytic lens—can be a valuable source of information, and
sometimes our only one.

Describing a 2003 panel, "Acting out and/or enactment", Perelberg
and Levinson (2003) write:

> Gail Reed [...] pointed out that currently the terms "enactment" and
> "acting out" are descriptive and denote communication by action
> rather than words. Reed felt that the different latent meanings of the
> two terms seem to "involve a good/bad dichotomy between theo-
> ries [one- versus two-person], analytic attitudes [countertransfer-
> entially disapproving versus reflective] and versions of the patient
> [obedient versus disobedient]." Reed questioned the need for two
> terms, preferring the term "acting out" with a more inclusive def-
> inition tied to being a manifestation of transference and severed
> from its topographic and energic definitions of tension reduction
> (as a resistance to memory). She proposed that there is often a ten-
> dency to use this term to institutionalise a defence against strong
> countertransference feelings. (pp. 153–154).

I believe that such countertransferential feelings often get confused
with the idea of proper analytic technique, leading analysts to not take
on, in analysis, patients like Mrs Green, who might need to express a
great deal through action before they can express it in words.

I find that if, as an analyst, I can provide an analytic space in which
the patient knows she can sit, stand, lie down, run around if need be,
speak, or not speak, be whatever and whoever she needs to be at a given
moment, that things then mostly start falling into place: not always as

expected, nor necessarily in ways that I am most comfortable with, but in a way that feels most authentic for the patient. Bromberg (2003) eloquently writes about this:

> If therapy is to provide a tranquil context for relived emotion—if we are to help transmute traumatic affect into a potential for "poetry"—what is needed? My answer is, a "safe-enough" inter-personal environment—one that has room for both the analyst's affective authenticity and an enacted replaying and symbolisation of early traumatic experience that does not blindly reproduce the original outcome. It is through this transmutation of trauma into "safe surprises" that, I believe, the dissociated ghosts of "not-me" are best persuaded, little by little, to cease their haunting and par-ticipate more and more actively and openly as affectively regulat-able, self-reflective aspects of "me." (p. 708)

Every action, symptom, and compromise formation is, of course, laden with multiple meanings, as Waelder pointed out decades ago. His classic paper, "The principle of multiple function", reprinted in *The Psychoanalytic Quarterly* (Waelder, 2007), is still refreshingly appro-priate for a further understanding of what my patient was attempting to deal with, through her use of the tape recorder during her sessions. Waelder writes:

> There are, then, eight problems whose solution is attempted by the ego: four of these are assigned to the ego and the other four the ego assigns to itself. [...] *It appears now as if our psychic life were directed by a general principle which we may name the principle of multiple function. According to this principle no attempted solution of a problem is possible which is not of such a type that it does not at the same time, in some way or other, represent an attempted solution of other problems.* Consequently, each psychic act can and must be conceived in every case as a simultaneous attempted solution of all eight problems, although it may be more successful as an attempted solution of one particular problem than of another. (pp. 78–79, italics added)

Our confusion regarding action, acting out, and enactment was sum-marised beautifully by Boesky (1982). He divides the concept of acting out into two distinct components, an unconscious transference fantasy and the related action or behaviour. He recognises the artificiality of separating the motor behavioural aspects of action from related fantasies and images. Further, he writes:

> Although the given instance of action may ostensibly serve to deny the fantasy which propels it, the action is always contextually linked to the fantasy. Here the defensive function of the action is to block awareness of painful affects which would ensue were there not an impedance to the further actualisation of the fantasy. In such instances the action may bear a relationship to the fantasy analogous in its function and complexity to the familiar relation between the manifest and latent dream (Grinberg, 1968; Mitscherlich-Nielsen, 1968). (p. 43)

Why did my patient feel she could not be with me unless she recorded what happened between us? Boesky (1982) asked precisely this question when he wrote, "It is this question—why does the patient substitute action for verbal communication?—which we least understand. Why do patients shift to action at all?" (p. 47). He adds, "Viewed from the angle of defence, clinical experience easily confirms that the shift to action serves to avoid unpleasant affect evoked by emerging transference fantasies in the 'here and now'" (ibid. p. 48).

We all know, however, that there are many patients who use actions, rather than words, to deal with transference fantasies or in the service of defence or resistance. Acknowledging this, Boesky writes:

> Obvious and profound differences separate those patients who cross this boundary rarely from those whose bustling traffic at this frontier is a source of bewilderment, and even danger. We want to know why certain patients can't tolerate average levels of frustration, and we assume that the patient's intolerance of painful affect is crucial in determining the shift of behaviour. This means we must account for the development of certain functional ego capacities and, therefore, developmental considerations are more important than dynamic issues (Beres, 1965). (Ibid. p. 51)

Boesky's question about why some patients frequently cross the boundary between words and actions is an excellent one. And what he postulated as possible reasons in his 1982 paper make profound sense. In the three decades since, analytic thinkers have moved even further in their attempts to understand how the mind works and why action might be a necessary—and, at times, the primary—route initially available to a patient for communication. In the introduction to their recently published edited volume, Levine et al. (2013) write:

> In the last several decades, the analytic field has widened considerably in scope. The therapeutic task is now seen by an increasing number of analysts to require that patient and analyst work together to strengthen, or to create, a psychic structure that was previously weak, missing, or functionally inoperative. This view, which may apply to all patients but is especially relevant to the treatment of non-neurotic patients and states of mind, stands in stark contrast to the more traditional assumption that the therapeutic task involves the uncovering of the unconscious dimension of a present pathological compromise formation that holds a potentially healthy ego in thrall. (p. 3)

Building on the work of others—including, but not limited to, Winnicott, Bion, Green, and Ferro—Levine (Levine & Brown, 2013) posits that sometimes "there is a failure or weakening of representation" in the mind, with "underlying issues and psychic states as not yet or only poorly articulable […] and therefore not yet interpretable and neither suitable nor available in their present state to form thoughts, to think with or about, or to be reflected upon" (p. 53). This is a fresh perspective on our understanding of what it is in the mind that pushes for expression via action, rather than reflection or words.

Making a clear distinction between states in which mental representations did once exist (but are temporarily erased because of certain psychological factors) and those in which representation never developed in the first place, Scarfone (2012) writes:

> There are indeed unconscious psychic strata where representations were erased […] disfigured by […] secondary repression. The blurring of the signs then resembles a famous tactic of the Venetians when Napoleon's army was getting near. […] [They] stripped the streets of their names to disorient the invaders. […] The manoeuvre certainly made things more complicated for the intruders, but the

streets and the maps were still there; it was therefore still possible to find one's way. (p. 4, italics added)

Scarfone goes on to remind us, however, that there are parts of the mind, even in seemingly neurotic patients:

> [...] where "something" presents itself without any corresponding psychical representation. In such quarters, the streets never had a name; actually, there are no real streets, but uncertain traces on trails difficult to thread. Nothing there finds an easy way towards the spoken word. (Ibid. p. 5)

How, then, do we, as analysts, decide where and how to intervene, and which route to follow, to be of greatest help to our patients? LaFarge (2000) clarifies:

> I contrast two aspects of the analyst's interchange with his patient. At one pole, I have placed the analyst's recognition of his patient's elaborated fantasies, often communicated by the patient in his verbal associations. The analyst feels this material to arise mainly from the patient, rather than from the analyst's own subjective experience. I have argued that this pole of the analytic situation often reflects the patient's experience of the analyst as a whole object and is often best understood within an ego-psychological frame of reference, in which interpretation is the chief therapeutic agent. At the other pole, I have placed the analyst's imaginative transformation of material that he feels mainly as arising within himself, as a shaping or a disturbance of his own subjective experience. I have argued that this second pole of the analytic situation often reflects the patient's experience of the analyst as a part object, conveyed in the patient's affects and actions rather than words. I have argued that this pole is often best understood within a Kleinian, or more specifically, a Bionian frame of reference, in which containment is an important therapeutic agent. From a theoretical standpoint, it might be argued that both the polarisation of two kinds of listening and the use of two theoretical frames, is unnecessary. As I have noted, the two poles rarely occur in pure form. The skilled analyst, whatever his theoretical frame, tends to draw upon both kinds of data, and to blend them in his formulations. And it has often

been argued that a good analyst who puts either of the two frames of reference that I attempt to integrate to full use will get a good clinical result. (pp. 81–82)

Patients like Mrs Green challenge the analyst to think deeper, reach higher, accept one's ignorance and the limitations of one's existing knowledge, and be prepared to learn from one's patient on the way to helping her. I am grateful for the lessons my patient taught me, the most significant being to remember that analytic technique is just that, a technique developed from a set of theories—and it requires constant revisiting as we continue to learn more and more from, and about, our patients.

CHAPTER FIVE

From an iPhone, through an iPad and an iMac, to the Cloud: the evolution of a sense of "I-ness"

Introduction

In this chapter I will present clinical material from a psychoanalytic treatment in which various "iMachines", now so readily available, became a conduit through which my patient's concerns about his sense of self (his I-ness) came into the analysis and could be worked with effectively. His associations about the iWorld allowed us deeper access into what he believed kept him from functioning more cohesively and solidly as a person, and enabled us to begin the process of working through the pain and sense of deprivation that had kept him stuck where he was.

In November 2008, in a cosy meeting room at La Sapinière—a charming resort in the Laurentian Mountains north of Montreal—I was presenting clinical material at a meeting of the Group for the Study of the Psychoanalytic Process (GSPP). The clinical material was from a session in which my patient was laughing at me about the way I pronounce certain words and my inability to pronounce certain letters of the English alphabet, such as "v" and "w", correctly. My patient then homed in on the fact that when I referred to his daughter Alicia, I emphasised both the "i" after the "l" and the "i" after the "c". This was incorrect, he added, but he had never told me this before because it tickled him to hear me make that mistake repeatedly. I asked what tickled him, and he replied that it made him feel I was not all together—that I too had certain foibles and problems, so that I made "Alicia" into Al-i-ci-a, which he pronounced "Al-i-sha", with the second "i" remaining silent.

I had thought about how similar his daughter's name sounded to mine ("Ai-sha"). I had also wondered about his light-hearted hostility in secretly laughing at me, rather than correcting me when I first made the mistake. The group added other thoughts about the material. Then one of the participants said that what was so striking was that *in the way I pronounced his daughter's name, I was giving her an "i" where none existed*, and he wondered what lay behind that. This was an exquisitely sensitive and perceptive insight, particularly since a large part of what my patient struggled with was his sense of terribly low self-worth and a feeling that he had to pretend to be someone other than who he really was—because who he really was could not possibly be acceptable to others or worth loving. To him, his seemingly powerful grandmothers, mother, and sisters were the ones who were self-assured and knew what they wanted and who they were. To get any attention, he had to go along with the program, so to speak, and admire them.

So when I mispronounced his daughter's name and added an "i" where none existed, his secret laughter at me was clearly a quiet revenge on "women who had all the power"—but was it also connected to a wish that I would help restore an "*I*", a real self of his own, to him? It was in this context that I shared with the group that my name was actually pronounced with two syllables and not three, as they had always pronounced it—i.e., "Eye-sha" or "Aye-sha", rather than "Ah-ee-sha". The members of the group were understandably dismayed and surprised to hear this, and asked why I hadn't told them before, given the fact that I had, by then, been a GSPP member for eight years. This took me, in my mind, to my identification with my patient and my struggles to find my own sense of myself (my I-ness), which had initially been connected to childhood events and losses and, later, to emigrating to the U.S. and having to discover a new sense of self—as a foreigner, an immigrant, and an immigrant parent of children born in America.

That meeting, in the fall of 2008, took place about a year after the first iPhone came onto the market. The link between iPhones and one's sense of self—and the iPhone as an extension of oneself—was already prominent, both in popular culture and in analytic sessions, where patients had started to bring in their iPhones to show me pictures, read emails they had sent or received, and, at times, to play messages that irate in-laws, bosses, friends, or co-workers had left. The analytic consulting room was alive with the sounds and sights of the iWorld, and this phenomenon only increased with time. My stance with this, as with most of what patients bring into their hours, was "Okay, we've just seen, read, or heard on your iPhone what you wanted to share with me. Now let's try to understand what it means to you to be able to tell me about it in this way, and what the content of what you've just shared with me means to you."

Clinical material

Mr Roth

Mr Roth, who was in his fifties, had been in analysis with me for about five years. His parents had gone through a bitter divorce when he was a young boy, and he had had great difficulty in establishing an intimate relationship. He was currently married, but struggled to feel close to his wife and often felt like a failure unless he was excelling at something, even a skill he was just beginning to learn.

Session 1

One morning, just in time for Mr Roth's session, I opened the door of my office suite (which is in my home) and walked outside to see whether he had arrived. He was sitting in his car in the parking area with the motor running. I waved to him and started to turn to go back inside. When he saw me, he got out of the car hurriedly and came into my office, visibly upset. He said that in his rush to come inside he had locked his keys in his car, and I acknowledged his distress and frustration. He first thought of calling his mother—who lived close by—to see whether she could help or had an extra set of keys to his car. He mused aloud that perhaps he could take her car to get the extra set of keys he kept at his home. I asked more about this, wondering about his feeling that only his mother could help at a time like this.

Mr Roth then realised it was not likely his mother would be able to be of real help, and wondered how he could call the American Automobile Association (AAA) to unlock his car. I was curious—and puzzled—as to why he had not asked if he could use my office phone to call AAA, and asked him about this. Mr Roth admitted that that would be the simplest and easiest thing to do, and reflected that it seemed rather casual—the kind of thing one might do at a friend's—and hence his worry about asking me, his analyst, if he could use my phone. He now asked if he could, and I said, "Yes, of course." Mr Roth then called AAA, came back to the couch, and lay down. He said he was feeling annoyed with himself for having made this stupid mistake, but felt relieved now that he had called AAA.

I noted that he was feeling relieved after having called an organisation that has one more "A" in its acronym than I have in my initials (AAA vs. AA). He laughed slightly—and, it seemed to me, self consciously—and said that they would be able to come by in about an hour, which would be after his session with me. In associating to why he might have done this, he recalled a conversation he had had with his mother the previous night that had really angered him. He felt she had been intrusive on the one hand, and, on the other, not really there for him, and said, "That's the way it's always been." I linked this to the transference in terms of how he experienced me as intrusive at times when I asked questions and his sense of my not being there for him when I went away on vacations or was quiet in the sessions.

At some point during the session he wondered how he would now communicate with AAA; they had said they would call him when they were close to my office. The problem was that his cell phone was also locked in his car. At the moment he had inadvertently locked the car with his cell phone and keys inside, he had been thinking about what had transpired between him and his mother and feeling very angry at her. It seemed quite clear that he had locked himself out as an expression of his guilt and his need to be punished. At the same time, he seemed to be expressing a wish to be rescued, and looked after, I thought. After he had stood up from the couch at the end of the session, he acknowledged his sense of helplessness as to how to communicate with AAA. He asked if I would be in the office and whether he could call from my office phone and give them that number, but I told him that I would be leaving the office right after I saw him. I found myself wondering what to do and finally decided to offer him my iPhone, which he could keep with him and give AAA as a contact number, since they were on their way.

Later that morning I went upstairs from my office, had breakfast, came back to my office, and saw that he had left my phone in the waiting room, as we had agreed. Apparently AAA had come and unlocked his car, and he had been able to drive off. The next day Mr Roth shared with me that he had found the iPhone fascinating; he had used it to locate AAA's phone number on the Internet. All he had to do was press the phone icon to dial the number. Privately, I thought that my iPhone had made AAA easily available to him. Was he wishing that I (AA) could be just as available—someone he could depend on who was just a phone call away? I attempted to understand what he felt about all of this, but with limited success.

A number of days later, however, Mr Roth told me in a rather shame-faced way that he had something to share with me. He said he'd been too embarrassed to talk to me about this, but felt that it was too impor-tant to *not* reveal it in his analysis. He told me that while he waited for AAA to arrive, after he had called them on my iPhone, he had tapped on the icon for photography and looked at pictures and a few videos I had stored. He had seen photographs of my family—one of me with my husband and our younger child and others of someone he imagined was my older daughter with a young man. They seemed very happy; it appeared that my daughter had found a companion she really enjoyed. Then he came across a video of my younger child and me, playing in the back yard with our dog, Riley. He thought it was the most heart-warming thing he had seen in a very long time, the way my young daughter and I were throwing toys to Riley and the way he would chase them.

He recalled a scene in the video in which Riley lay on the grass and refused to play the game any longer. At some point I had laugh-ingly said to him, "Come on, lazy bones, come get your toy!" Mr Roth thought that maybe I was being mean to my dog. Then he recalled that later in the video, he heard me calling tenderly to Riley: "Hey, googly eyes, we're having lots of fun with you."

Mr Roth started crying profusely when speaking about this, saying that it made him feel so envious of the children I had, the family I had, and the love they got from me. It made him feel that my children must be growing up, or had grown up, with a strong sense of self. I said at this point that he seemed to be saying that he thought my children had a good sense of their I-ness because of the love they had received from their mother—something he felt he had missed in his life and that had contributed to his lack of a sturdy sense of himself who could and would be loved, no matter what.

I wondered with him if he was afraid that I would not like him anymore, now that he had looked at the photographs and videos on my iPhone, which I had given him so that he could be in contact with AAA. "Perhaps you think AA will think you want too much from her?" I asked. He started crying again and said he felt really ashamed of himself for having done this. He wasn't sure what came over him, but he'd felt very curious. By the time he had looked through all the photographs and videos and AAA had arrived, he had been sitting next to the parking area, crying and feeling sad for himself and envious of the good things that he felt went on in my home. I thought that perhaps he had wanted to look at my photos and videos as a way to satisfy his deep curiosity about me and his wish to get close to me; looking through the pictures on my iPhone had allowed him to do that without letting me know how much he wanted such closeness. We also talked about his feeling deeply touched that I had given him my iPhone to help him in a way he felt a good mother might.

I was not unaware that his looking at my private photos and videos might have many other meanings—some hostile, some sexual, some having to do with wanting me to know what it felt like to be intruded upon (as he had experienced with his parents), and some, perhaps, even related to wanting me to feel jarred and betrayed. I thought, however, that the other aspects would come to light in good time. In the immediacy of the moment, I was most impressed by his hunger to have more of me—his yearning to have me, AA, available to him as easily as AAA could be summoned; his attack on himself for wishing to know more about me and to have more of me; his envy; and his terror that I would dislike him, as he disliked himself, for being so needy, curious, and envious.

* * *

In the almost two-month interval between the session described above and the session that follows, Mr Roth bought an iPhone. This purchase was very much linked to his feelings about my having an iPhone and seeing all that an iPhone allowed one to accomplish (e.g., connect easily with others, such as AAA, in times of need; record memories; store data; and note important dates on the calendar). A little later he purchased an iPad, feeling that this would make him more effi-cient and his life more organised; he also used an iMac he had bought six years earlier. We continued to work, both with the reality of what these devices were able to do for him and with the deeper meanings of what he wanted—and hoped to have—in his life, as a result of using these iDevices.

Session 2

Mr Roth began talking, with some embarrassment, about how much time he had wasted over the weekend because of problems with electronics. He had realised that his electronic calendar was all messed up; on the calendar on his computer, Thursdays were totally empty. He was horrified when he realised this; he had been backing up the calendar on his iPhone to his iMac, but obviously it had not worked. He went to the Apple store and was told that the problem was that his iMac was not compatible with his iPhone and his new iPad. "Even when I was backing up," he explained to me, "I was not synchronising; they are two different functions." So that all of his devices would be compatible, he bought a new iMac.

I noticed he was speaking very fast, with anxiety and embarrassment, and asked about this. He said he was embarrassed because he and I had recently had a conversation about his having gotten mixed up about a session he thought we had scheduled, which we had not; we were supposed to meet later that day, but he had not changed the time in his calendar. He was embarrassed that with all of his electronic gadgets, he still couldn't keep track of appointments correctly—whereas I used a paper calendar, as did Dr Turk (an internist and male friend of mine whom Mr Roth also knew socially), and we both seemed to get along quite well. I said Mr Roth seemed ashamed, as though Dr Turk and I had some special capacity he did not and could never have. I asked what he imagined allowed us to function well with our paper calendars and what made it difficult for him to do so, with the many good gadgets he had at his disposal?

He began to describe how, if he were better able to not only back up, *but also synchronise*, data from all his different iDevices to the Cloud, it would ultimately free up more space—more memory—in his computer's hard drive. I tried to clarify: "So what you're saying is that the Cloud, if properly used, allows you to synchronise events or data recorded on your iPhone, iPad, and iMac?" He said, "Exactly!" He explained that there was a "Cloud," and that it was in Colorado. "It's not a big cloud. It's a building that houses computers, and each person who is using iPhones, iPads, iMacs, etc., has a slice of the Cloud." His slice was 5 gigabytes; if he wanted more, he would have to buy it. If properly done, data from all his devices could be synchronised—when he backed up the calendar from his iPhone or iPad, for instance, and it was stored on the Cloud, all of his devices, including his computer, would be in synchrony. This would then allow him to be able to access his calendar on the iMac, if somebody called him when he was home and working on it. Without checking his iPhone or iPad, he could easily know what was happening. "Your life would all be more synchronised," I remarked. "That's what you feel is missing."

I was struck by the beautiful imagery in Mr Roth's descriptions. My mind went to how mothers who are involved and helpfully engaged manage, with their calendars, a young child's numerous school, music, sports, social, and family commitments. Often the child simply has to ask such a mother and, like a good Cloud, she—the synchroniser of all the data of his life—can tell him where he needs to be when. He will not have to worry about such details until he is older. Such mothering during childhood, I thought, helps create the space and freedom in the child's mind and life—like freed-up space on a computer's hard drive—for growth and creativity. When the child's mind is not cluttered with the need to remember and manage too much too early—or the anxiety of having to be an adult too soon—then, safe in the knowledge that there is a good parental Cloud who will store his data and be his memory and synchroniser, the child can revel in the pleasures of childhood and, when he is truly ready to do so, more ably take on the functions of remembering and synchronising.

I emerged from my musings; Mr Roth was speaking. He had many feelings about how I seemed to be able to do all of this well and without the need for so many gadgets, while he had spent more than $1,000 over the weekend trying to perfect his electronic network. I told Mr Roth that I thought he was telling us that what was missing in him—what made it difficult for him to synchronise parts of himself and his life—were certain aspects of what could be described as "I-ness". He felt, I said, that there were parts of himself that could not be synchronised or brought together because he had not had enough (or consistent) experiences of having a Cloud—a good parental cloud—over him that would absorb all the stuff that had been thrown at him during his childhood. Such a parental cloud would function to take this material, help him sort it out, store it, and deal with it in a way that did not mess up his hard drive. I also spoke about the idea that it was heartbreaking for him to have to pay (in the form of his analytic fee) to have a slice of a well functioning "Cloud".

I was referring here to the idea that the various stimuli that came at him during his childhood had felt overwhelming and created a sense of internal disorganisation, particularly during and after his parents' divorce, when there had been fights, emotional upheaval, and financial problems. There had not been a consistently good-enough caretaker to help him sort through the tumultuous experiences of his childhood and make sense of them—or render them less toxic—so that they could be stored in his mind in a meaningful and coherent way, rather than in a way that made him feel overwhelmed. At that point he started crying and said that that was exactly it; *that* was what he felt I had and Dr Turk had—and perhaps, in some way, we had it together (Mr Roth knew that Dr Turk and I, though at least a generation apart in age, were good friends).

I recalled with him that over the last several sessions he had been speaking a lot about his father and his pain about their difficult and poor relationship. Mr Roth had spoken with great pain about how unavailable, as a helpful figure in his life, his father was; instead, his father had to be constantly rescued by Mr Roth. I said it sounded as though he felt that Dr Turk and I were like a good father-son pair who helped each other—that Dr Turk helped me with my I-ness. Mr Roth said he thought perhaps each of us helped the other with their I-ness, because we loved each other. After a pause, he spoke of being in the lobby of a nearby art movie theatre a few days earlier. Dr Turk had also been there, and had crossed the room to talk to Mr Roth and say it was good to see him. Mr Roth had responded that it was good to be *seen*.

After that, Dr Turk looked across the room thoughtfully and they were quiet together; it seemed as if they didn't have any more to say. Mr Roth found himself thinking that if I had been there, Dr Turk and I would have had a lot to say to each other. I said, "As though our iPhones, iPads, and iMacs would all be synchronised and coordinated." He started crying again, and said, "I really do feel that you and he have that in you. Something's helped you with that capacity of synchronising and putting things together. Even what you said to me just now, a little bit earlier in the session, the way you brought together my rambling thoughts about all these electronics and the way you made sense of it, and then helped *me* make sense of it—all of that is a capacity you have that I don't."

I responded gently, "And you are glad I can use that capacity in me to help you, but you're also envious I have it in the first place, right?" He said yes, that often I had talked to him about this in terms of what he felt he lacked from his mother, growing up, but today it did seem to be more about his father, the lack of this organising capacity, and I had understood even that! He was glad I could help him, sure, but it made him feel so bitter. He had thought at times that I must have been helped by my analyst: "Maybe he was your good Cloud!" What he really believed, though, was that whatever my analyst gave me was only an addition to what I must have already received from my mother and father.

At this point he referred to a talk he had heard me give at an open house for the psychoanalytic institute. "You told the audience this story about how your father tried to convince you to go into medicine, rather than letting you study English literature—but you know what?" With pain in his voice, he said, "At least you had a father who *cared*, who talked with you." I said I could understand how painful it was for him when he realised how detached his father was from him. And I thought of the difference between a big, fluffy cloud and the powerful, magical Cloud that can store data, retain memory, and synchronise life events. This was what Mr Roth felt he had missed with both parents—but, at this point in the analysis, even more so with his father.

Discussion

Brief overview of pertinent literature

Electronic computers came out in the 1950s (though mass/commercial production did not take off until the 1960s and 1970s), the Internet became commercialised in 1995, and the first iPhone was launched in 2007. These devices, which have radically altered the nature of communication, are now part of our—and our patients'—day-to-day lives. Over the last few years, psychoanalysts (e.g., Akhtar, 2011) have started to be interested not only in how such technology is used by, and affects, our patients, but also in the impact it has had on the analytic process.

In this regard, Kantrowitz (2009) writes:

> The internet's growth and its interactions with the mind are coming into analytic focus as individuals find psychological uses for this new tool while simultaneously adapting to its functions. Understanding these dynamics, their impact on the analytic dyad, and the resulting new positions of the psychoanalyst is of increasing importance as the internet's existence integrates further into our culture and our individual lives. (p. 979)

Patients and analysts are texting each other, communicating via email, and participating in treatment not only by telephone, but also, increasingly, via Skype; even the naysayers are finally acknowledging that technology need not be seen as an impediment to psychoanalysis. Meanwhile, those of us who have already embraced these new forms of communication believe that we must begin studying what is being stirred up in treatment as technology begins to mix with traditional forms of analytic discourse. In her report on a panel on Internet interaction between analysts and patients, Kantrowitz (2009) writes that panel member Kimberlyn Leary:

> [...] stressed the concept of the internet as composed of "cyberplaces." Different aspects of the internet carry different rules, much as one would find in any collection of cultures. The alterations noted in moving from cyberplace to cyberplace can involve questions of what is public and what is private, or what is surface and what is deep. In these numerous realms, multiple identities seem to coexist. New selves are brought into these places, and as a result we see shifts in our work as clinicians and analysts.
>
> *Because psychoanalysis has a practiced understanding of the intersubjective, it is in a unique position to understand the new modalities arising as a result of the internet and its many interfaces and boundaries with the external world.* (p. 987, italics added)

Leary, with her usual keenness, underscores that analysts are in a special position to study what we, and our patients, might be expressing through the interface between the Internet and the external world. Such study can greatly inform us about our own internal world and that of our patients.

In his compelling book, *The Shallows: What the Internet is Doing to Our Brains*, Carr (2010) refers to parents' concerns when, in the 1970s, students were allowed to use calculators for math: they were afraid that their children would not retain a strong grasp of basic mathematical concepts. Their fear, however, proved to be unwarranted; as Carr writes, "the calculator made it easier for the brain to transfer ideas from working memory to long-term memory and encode them" (p. 193). The Web, however,

> [...] has a very different effect. It places *more pressure* on our working memory, not only diverting resources from our higher reasoning faculties but obstructing the consolidation of long-term memories and the development of schemas. The calculator, a powerful but highly specialised tool, turned out to be an aid to memory. The Web is a technology of forgetfulness. (Ibid. p. 193)

Turkle's (2011) deeply researched book, *Alone Together: Why We Expect More from Technology and Less from Each Other*, is one of the most thoughtful texts I have read on the relationship between humans and the machines we use for communication and these technologies' impact on our relationships with others. She writes:

> In interviews with young and old, I find people genuinely terrified of being cut off from the "grid." People say that the loss of a cell phone can "feel like a death." [...] Whether or not our devices are in use, without them, we feel disconnected, adrift. (p. 16)

This raises the possibility that these devices, and in particular the iMachines, have become, for many, an extension of the self. Furthermore, regarding the paradox created by our heavy use of technology to connect and communicate, Turkle (2011) writes:

> Most of the time, we carry that technology with us. In fact, being alone can start to seem like a precondition for being together because it is easier to communicate if you can focus, without interruption, on your screen. In this regime, a train station [...] is no longer a communal space but a place of social collection: people come together but do not speak to each other. [...] The hopscotch boxes are gone. The kids are out, but they are on their phones. (p. 155)

And she asks, *"What is a place if those who are physically present have their attention on the absent?"* (ibid. pp. 156–157, italics added). Her question is a good segue into a deeper understanding of Mr Roth's material.

Further thoughts on the clinical material

As we have seen repeatedly in clinical material presented throughout this book, patients tell us about themselves in many different ways. Mr Roth told me about his struggle to develop a solid, organised, cohesive sense of himself through his journey into the world of iMachines, with which he was attempting to develop and master functions he had not been able to previously—because his important objects were, to paraphrase Turkle, physically present but with their attention on the absent. In the case of his parents, this was not due to technology, but because of their unresolved traumatic pasts—with which they remained over-involved, to their children's detriment.

By a solid, organised, cohesive sense of self, I do not mean a self in which there are no contradictions, weaknesses, or conflicts. Quite the contrary. I believe that Mr Roth's idealised image of me (and Dr Turk) as having it all together was a mirror image of what he expected from *himself* in order to feel all together. So, for him, the journey we began with the sessions described above took us to places in which we worked hard together so that he could not only mourn what he felt he hadn't gotten from his parents, but also recognise that even those who *did* get enough from their parents do not automatically have selves that consistently function well. And that it is precisely this knowledge—and the fact that one feels well loved, despite being imperfect—that gives rise to a sturdy sense of self.

In his chapter in *The Mother and Her Child: Clinical Aspects of Attachment, Separation, and Loss*, Akhtar (2012) describes twelve tasks a mother performs for a child to facilitate development. He is mindful that such a listing could be reductionist and artificial, since, as he notes, "the whole is greater than the sum of its parts". Nonetheless, the list is helpful. The tasks are holding; containing; protecting and nourishing; awakening the libidinal potential of the child's body; introducing the child to his or her inner world; evoking the core self and helping consolidate gender identity; seeing goodness in the child; imparting ego skills; surviving; letting go of the child; remaining available as a psychological "home base"; and helping the child bear the oedipal situation and teaching the child to respect the father (pp. 2–10). Akhtar adds that "the child's own drive for mastery and the father's pulling the child out of the infantile symbiotic orbit and into the world of external events also play an important role" (ibid. p. 7).

In thinking about what was going on in Mr Roth's analysis during the tumultuous weeks described above, it seems to me that by responding as I did—i.e., to what he had done with my iPhone—I was providing for him, neither for the first time in the analysis nor the last, many of the above functions. And it was not a coincidence that in the later material, the father's role figured prominently. This was a cycle that was repeated frequently in the analysis, as Mr Roth worked through the after-effects of a painful and emotionally disorganised childhood.

I could not have known, when I gave Mr Roth my iPhone to use while he waited for AAA, that such a fascinating and useful sequence of events and associations would emerge from a brief interaction that involved an electronic device. I am reminded here of the last lines of Kantrowitz's (2009) report: "Regardless of one's assumptions and perceptions of online technology and all its cyberplaces, the effects are large and are being felt everywhere, even in our offices. Rather than turn away from these, we must view them as new realities to be understood" (p. 988).

PART IV

WHEN POLITICAL EVENTS INTRUDE
UPON CLINICAL SPACE

Sadistic transferences in the context of ethnic difference: before and after 9/11

Introduction

In each analytic dyad, the analyst and the patient can differ in numerous ways. Even when they belong to similar racial, ethnic, or religious groups, significant differences can exist that sometimes never get talked about. To understand the meaning these dissimilarities have for a patient and how he or she uses them, starting with the most superficial and accessible and moving toward the deepest underpinnings, is one of the tasks of an analysis. In this chapter, I will discuss sadistic transferences expressed toward me by three male patients. These transferences were superficially linked to my ethnicity (a Muslim from Pakistan), their feelings about it, and the difference it created between us. In each analysis, however, the deeper and more personal meanings of this sadism were revealed over time. I will focus both on how *my* analytic functioning changed and deepened in the aftermath of "9/11"[1] (which allowed me to recognise and work with my patients' sadism more helpfully) and how the material *patients* brought into their analyses with me was profoundly affected and altered by the events of 9/11 and the regional and world events that followed—a sociopolitical reality that became woven into patients' expression of personal conflicts.

Let me place this chapter in context. At the 1997 winter meetings of the American Psychoanalytic Association, I presented a paper (Abbasi, 1997) entitled "When worlds collide in the analytic space: aspects of a 'cross-cultural' psychoanalysis", which was based on my work with Mr Brodsky a young Jewish man and recent immigrant to America, who had deep-felt and negative reactions to his "discovery" that his female analyst was also a Muslim. In that paper, I described what Mr Brodsky and I understood about the personal sources of his hatred toward me as a Muslim woman as it related to his early, conflicted relationships with his mother and sister. I also described the poignant similarities we discovered in the midst of our considerable differences: we were fellow immigrants mourning for the motherland and struggling to develop a hybrid identity as we settled into our new country. Further, I wrote about these issues as they manifested themselves in my own analysis with a male, Jewish analyst and a male, Jewish supervisor who was helping me in my work with Mr Brodsky. In 1998, I contributed a chapter (Abbasi, 1998) entitled "Speaking the unspeakable" for *Blacks and Jews on the Couch*, temporarily finding safety in addressing a conflict that was not related to Muslims.

Then, in September 2001, Muslim terrorists attacked America, killing almost 3,000 people and changing, forever, much about the world we live in. For a few years I busied myself writing book reviews. Many years later, I wrote a chapter (Abbasi, 2008) entitled "'Whose side are you on?': Muslim psychoanalysts treating non-Muslim patients" for *The Crescent and the Couch: Cross-Currents Between Islam and Psychoanalysis*, in which I detailed the rage, distrust, and terror two female analytic patients had felt toward me, their Muslim analyst, in the aftermath of 9/11. And finally, in 2010, I wrote a paper (Abbasi, 2012) entitled "'A very dangerous conversation': The patient's internal conflicts elaborated through the use of ethnic and religious differences between analyst and patient", which was based on my recent work with a Jewish man whose most disturbing aspects of himself were brought into the analysis by way of the Jewish-Muslim rifts and differences that made up the news of the day.

To present a comparison of my work with patients before and after 9/11, with particular focus on the patients' sadistic feelings in the transference, I will present (in condensed form) my treatment of Mr Brodsky, followed by process material from two other analyses.

Clinical material

Mr Brodsky

Mr Brodsky, a Jewish man in his thirties, came to see me in the early years of my analytic career and several years before the events of 2001. He reported great difficulty with feelings of rage, which resulted in terrible arguments with his wife. His childhood had been marked by a father who had been successful as a businessman early in the patient's childhood, but then sold the business and failed at all other careers, which was witnessed by Mr Brodsky from the age of ten onwards. He had a younger brother and sister and felt that his sister was his parents' favourite. His mother often complained to him about how inadequate his father was as a provider. Mr Brodsky came to America in his teens, went to college, joined the human resources department of a company, and married a well-educated Jewish woman whose professional development was hindered by her emotional issues, which seemed to concern Mr Brodsky—but also made him feel superior to his wife.

He responded to my recommendation for a five-times-a-week analysis on the couch by citing time and financial constraints and began, instead, a four-times-a-week analysis, sitting up. Over the next few months, Mr Brodsky talked in sessions in a very controlled and controlling way, condescendingly remarking upon my "good work" when I said something that felt useful to him, and wondering how his sitting up was affecting my progression as a new psychoanalytic candidate. He expressed sympathy for the difficult situation I must be in with my supervisor over this matter. In an analytically dutiful way, I asked him his thoughts about all of this but gradually realised that I felt angry, inadequate, controlled, and paralysed as an analyst with him.

I could now point out to him that he seemed to feel that I had more to lose than he did if he was not fully helped in his analysis. What was *that* about? Memories emerged of his being held between his mother's knees when he was six and a female friend of hers giving him a shot in the buttock. "I can't use the couch," he said, "because you want me to." He then told me that when he was a teenager he had tried to physically attack his mother during a fight and had to be held back by two people. In another incident he had pointed a rifle at his sister, and most recently, before coming to see me, he had kicked his wife in the buttocks (the very part of his body where he had been injected by his mother). His recalling these events in this particular sequence allowed me to share with him my thought that he was afraid that I wanted to humiliate and control him, and was protecting himself by putting me down and controlling the structure of his analysis even if it kept him from using the treatment in the most valuable way. These discussions allowed Mr Brodsky to begin coming five times a week, still sitting up. Now his discomfort about feeling attracted to me and experiencing me as his desirable, dark-haired older sister came into the analysis, with worries that he might feel sexually aroused and at my mercy if he were to use the couch.

The greatest shift emotionally, however, was centred on an external event: the Israeli–Palestinian peace accord of 1993, trumpeted in newspapers all over the world by the image of the historic handshake between Yasser Arafat and Yitzhak Rabin. On the day this news broke, Mr Brodsky brought it up in the session and then could not speak. We then learned that even though he knew I was from Pakistan, he had not allowed himself to "know" I was a Muslim. All hell now broke forth in the analysis, in a way that ultimately proved to be critically useful. Mr Brodsky shared with me, with great trepidation, that in school in his early years in America, he had been an active member of a Jewish political group and had organised many anti-Arab and anti-Muslim rallies. His favourite rabbi used to call Muslims "dogs", and he had been raised to believe that all Muslims were anti-Semites. "I must see", he said, "that we could not possibly work together."

I found myself feeling intrigued by and curious about his responses, but not particularly disturbed; the war between the Muslims and the Jews felt like a remote and distant problem. What, I thought privately, did *I* have to do with that conflict, really? I had grown up in Pakistan, entire countries away from the Middle Eastern struggle between the Israeli Jews and the Palestinian Muslims. Since my patient was struggling with these issues, however, and they were very much a part of his personal experience and history, I would certainly try my best to help him with these matters. In retrospect, *it is precisely this lack of internal disturbance on my part, and my attempts to distance myself geographically and emotionally from the conflicts my patient was describing, that should have alerted me that something was amiss with me.*

Instead, I simply said to Mr Brodsky, quite calmly, that I heard his distrust of me as a Muslim and a possible anti-Semite, his terror of his own hatred and rage, and his fear of mine. But why was it that we could not continue to talk about all of this? He replied thoughtfully that even though we were so different, he felt that I had always been very decent with him; maybe he would be crazy to stay, but perhaps leaving would be foolish. So we continued, Mr Brodsky and I, external "enemies" engaged in a psychoanalytic process, with the common goal of helping him understand his own suffering.

Sometime after this I changed my car, going from a stripped-down Nissan Centra to a more luxurious Audi. My Nissan used to make Mr Brodsky feel that I must be an unsuccessful physician, just as his father had been an unsuccessful businessman. My German Audi was "a lovely colour, a great car," he said, "but I would never buy one like that. I call it a Nazi car." I could now interpret more openly Mr Brodsky's anxieties about what each of us—a male and a female, a Jew and a Muslim—might do to the other were he to deepen his analysis. He now shared with me that in part, his not using the couch made him feel like he had fooled his wife, whom he felt had coerced him into "going into analysis". He felt he was avenging himself by paying to see me but not using the couch: "I'm fooling her. She thinks I am really in analysis, but I'm sort of in and sort of not." I asked, "And how about the way in which you are fooling and hurting yourself?" He said he was only now beginning to see that a little bit. These exchanges between us led Mr Brodsky to use the couch for the first time, nine months into the analysis. The importance of those nine months, the period of gestation, and his wish for me to "carry" him as the good-enough mother he had never had, was not lost on either of us.

In the latter part of the third year of Mr Brodsky's analysis, I needed to stop working on Saturdays, which was one of the days I used to see him. I talked with him about this to see if we could find another time during the week. His reaction was strong and vivid. There was much curiosity about the change and anger about how inconvenient this would be for him. Gradually, associations emerged about the dark-skinned maid who had worked at his house when he was a child. She cleaned the house every weekday, but never came on weekends. I wondered about the derogatory implication of my being "paid help" and wondered whether this was a way for him to deal with his feelings of helplessness and anger about my unavailability over the weekend. He then told me that he had not had a close relationship with this maid; like his mother, she seemed to prefer his sister and his brothers over him. As we talked about this and its link to his current feelings of feeling unimportant with me, he was able to set up a fifth time with me during the week.

A couple of sessions after this, however, he came in on a Monday and told me that something very upsetting had happened over the week-end. He had a cat, which had been his pet since he came to the U.S., that he kept in the garage because his wife did not like it. He had never had the cat declawed, and it liked to kill small animals and bring them into the garage. Over the weekend, the cat had attacked a small rabbit and brought it into the garage. The rabbit was still alive, even though the cat had bitten a chunk of flesh out of it, and his wife had pleaded with him to kill the rabbit quickly. Mr Brodsky spent quite some time in the back yard deciding how best to do this. Ultimately, he used a shovel to smash the rabbit's head.

As Mr Brodsky spoke, I became aware that his affect seemed to be one of both fear and excitement. I also noticed that in his "debating" the various merits and demerits of the options available to him for putting the rabbit out of its misery, he had, of course, prolonged its agony. Later that night, at the moment he was about to have intercourse with his wife, she suddenly asked him if he was going to get rid of the cat. He had felt very angry with her, he told me, and turned away. He added, "I think my analysis must be helping. At another point in the past I would have been tempted to throw her out of the bed, but I didn't. I just turned away from her." I noted the violently angry feelings he had toward his wife when he felt she was hitting him "below the belt". I noted also the difficulty he had in putting the rabbit out of its misery, thus prolonging its suffering (an act of sadism, I thought privately). I pointed out the context in which these associations had emerged, a context that was connected to my being unavailable to him over the weekend.

Mr Brodsky then began to talk about a Muslim woman he had dated in college in the U.S. He said he had "forgotten" to tell me about this. This was a woman he had known for about a year but never had sex with, because she refused to have a physical relationship with him. He had been strongly attracted to her, but could not get anywhere with her. During the next few days he talked of his concern about my being alone in the office early in the morning when he came to see me. He said he was worried I would be attacked and raped in the parking lot and he described fantasies of how he would save me. I noted his concern for me, but said that interestingly, he was concerned for me in this fantasy after placing me in a position of danger. It seemed he was struggling enormously with his feelings of needing to protect me *and* his feelings of wanting to hurt me. After a pause he said he wondered how my husband could allow me to come to the office so early in the morning and that perhaps my husband had divorced me because of my professional goals and ambitions. His thoughts then went to being about ten years old and finding love letters written to his father by a woman with whom his father had been having an affair. He had given these letters to his mother, but, much to his surprise, his mother had not left his father, even though there had been tremendous fights at home between them. His mother had been very angry at him for having told her about this. He felt enraged that she did not appreciate what he had done and had not left his father, about whom she was always complaining.

I noted with Mr Brodsky that he seemed to want me to have been abandoned by my husband or to have left my husband because of him—to create a separation in my marriage of the kind that had not occurred in his parents' failed marriage, even after he revealed his father's infidelity to his mother. I noted how important it was to him to be important to me and the lengths to which he had to go in his fantasies to achieve this—how unsure he felt of his position with me.

Further associations now began to include thoughts about an affair he had had with a married woman (a white American) after he had first moved to the U.S. He described her as being several years older than he and living with her husband and children. She had helped him in many ways in the first few years of being in a country that was foreign to him. One day she came to his apartment after a party, and they made love. Afterward, as she was sleeping with her head on his shoulder, he put his arm around her neck and started bending his forearm, trying to strangle her. After a few moments of doing this he felt "shocked and scared". I said, "Perhaps you recognised how close you came to killing her, and how much that troubled you?" He said, with much feeling, "I loved her and hated her. I loved her for everything she was and what she did for me and I hated her because she was never fully mine. She always had her own life." I asked, "Like your mother?" and he responded, angrily and with vigour, "Damn you, yes, and like you. And like my sister."

This conversation led to his telling me in great detail, over time, about his beautiful sister, who was accomplished at everything and had a host of admirers following her around. "I felt," Mr Brodsky said bitterly, "like a little puppy shadowing her." I remembered with a sense of shock that he had told me early in our work that his favourite rabbi used to say that all Muslims were dogs. I brought this up with him, and he said, somewhat self-consciously, but with relief, "So that makes you just like me, I guess, a puppy, a worthless dog who follows people around." I said, "And perhaps also a bitch?" He laughed and responded, "Thank you—actually, yes, I do feel that way sometimes, especially when you have to change my times or cancel a session."

I reflected with him that he had a constant struggle in his mind, between loving and needing a woman and feeling enraged at not having his needs met by her. This created in him not just a sense of anger and rage, but the urge to kill—like his cat, who lived in the garage and killed little animals. My unavailability to him over the weekend seemed to have precipitated the same feeling: that I did not need him as much as he needed me—like his mother, who had chosen to stay with a violent, unfaithful husband while scolding the patient for having caused problems, and the older married woman who stayed with her husband but maintained a sexual relationship with him. The violent cat, I said, with the sharp claws represented an aspect of him, one that worried and frightened him although he felt he could not survive without it. A few weeks after this he started trying to find a home for the cat, and a few months later he gave it away.

We continued to work together, and from time to time his sharp claws would come out again—when he told me he could not increase my fee, for instance, but was giving money to a Jewish charity, or when he wondered whether I would successfully graduate from my analytic training if he were to quit his analysis. We were more able to relate such sadistic attacks on me to his need to deny *his* helplessness and dependence *and* his satisfaction at feeling he had rendered me helpless or was hurting me. Over the course of the analysis, we came to understand much about how Mr Brodsky's perceptions of me were intricately connected, primarily, to his feelings about his mother and sister, by whom he had felt excluded and hurt and toward whom he felt great rage—rage that was, initially, easier to experience as the righteous, politically determined rage of a Jew towards a Muslim rather than a deep and personally felt rage toward me as a controlling, withholding mother and the sister he loved, wanted, and hated. This, in turn, allowed us to examine his complicated feelings about his father and brother.

How I changed as an analyst after 9/11

To say that the terrible events of 9/11 and their aftermath affected all of us in profound ways does not do justice to the enormity of what happened. On my part, knowing that Muslims had caused such destruction in my adopted country and killed so many innocent people was shocking and, at first, surprising: how could these be "my people"? Was I really one of "those people"? And who, actually, were "my people"? For the first time since my emigration to the U.S. in 1987, I began to realise that I was both an American and foreign to America. In a tentative way, I struggled to understand more of what this event had evoked in me. External events bring forth different responses from each one of us, responses that are rooted in our personal life histories. The fact that America was connected to a deeply painful, life-altering event in my childhood, and that America was also the country I had adopted as my home in my late twenties—and where I had become a psychoanalyst—took on new and more complex meanings after 9/11. The recognition that my struggle to sort out my alliances and where I belonged was related to childhood struggles—over splits, factions, and divided loyalties in my family of origin—took much longer and is an ongoing effort; as such matters are for most of us.

Then there was, of course, the professional aspect. As an immigrant Muslim analyst of Pakistani origin, my work life took an unexpected turn. My patients started to bring in their intense fear—and hatred—of Muslims, while turning to me, a Muslim, for help with the terror of their own rage toward the terrorist Muslims (and all that they represented). I was put in the curious and difficult position of trying to quickly find my own precarious balance about the events of 9/11 and, at the same time, help my patients find theirs. The devastation caused by the terrorist attacks had breached the necessary boundary between fantasy and reality to a shocking degree, and the "as-if" quality of my patients' transferences toward me was temporarily shattered. They vacillated between imagining, on the one hand, that I was a reliable analyst toward whom they could have destructive wishes, *feeling* that I might retaliate but at the same time knowing, on a deeper level, that I would not, and on the other, feeling that I was an unreliable and dangerous person who came of dangerous stock, and that their hateful feelings toward me might actually cause me to hurt them: after all, look at what my people had just done.

On my part, the sadism and viciousness of the terrorist attacks made old external experiences and my internal responses to them come alive in a way that was new and useful, but also frightening. The "terrorist" parts of me seemed temporarily too real, and in my mind, the boundary between what was fantasy and what was reality felt strained, reminiscent of childhood conflicts.

I listened to my patients, knowing that I was not functioning at my best as an analyst, and tried to sort out my own feelings, while also feeling a need to help my patients, who were distressed and frightened. Together we navigated the turbulent seas where prejudice, rooted in the innermost recesses of our minds, reigns supreme and threatens to temporarily obscure the search for meaning. I was forced to become more honest with myself, as I struggled to deal with some of my patients' vitriolic attacks against "my" people. How had I managed to deal with Mr Brodsky relatively calmly, I now wondered, unfazed by his initial attacks on me as a Muslim, only later understanding that they derived from his personal conflicts? I had thought it was because of my great capability to not take things personally. I now realised that it was because I had been what might be best described as the opposite of the "James Bond martini style" of analyst: shaken, not stirred. I had felt stirred, intrigued by, and curious about Mr Brodsky—but, defensively, had *not* allowed myself to be shaken to the core, to be sufficiently disturbed by him. Yet this is a prerequisite for every truly useful analytic process.

In the wake of 9/11, I also questioned my previously naïve belief that another reason Mr Brodsky's attacks on me as a Muslim had not bothered me was because I had never met a Jewish person until I came to the U.S. at the age of twenty six. What was so alive for him—the danger of our differences—was supposedly not a problem for me. Yet how was this possible? I had grown up in a country where the government and the media clearly sided with the Palestinian Muslims whenever the Israeli–Palestinian issue was discussed. The same was true of discussions I heard at home. I had believed I had no shred of anti-Semitism in me—but now I questioned that belief. I began to take a deeper look at my own prejudice, its origins and meanings. Which one of us does not have secret prejudices, often connected to our early experiences, which we compartmentalise into neatly rationalised categories? And wasn't this what many of my patients were struggling to sort out for themselves in the wake of an external reality that had caused extreme damage and loss and reawakened internal turmoil, albeit somewhat differently in each person?

I will now present process material from the analyses of two male patients I worked with after 9/11.

Mr Sullivan

Mr Sullivan, who began his analysis in 2008, was a young and successful financial adviser. One of four children, he had been raised in a Catholic family, having attended parochial schools and gone to church regularly. His father, an attorney, seemed cold, disinterested, and unavailable to Mr Sullivan during his childhood. Worse, the father would at times brutally beat Mr Sullivan and his brother, usually because his mother reported the boys' wrongdoings to their father. His two sisters were spared these beatings, and Mr Sullivan grew to resent and hate them, both because they were protected from the physical violence and because they seemed to get the kind of attention from his mother that he craved. As he entered his early twenties, he moved out on his own and stopped practicing his religion, feeling that Catholicism and the Catholic church were simply reminders of his painfully brutal past. He came for treatment after the second woman he had been engaged to broke off their engagement, complaining that he was very controlling. He decided to consult with me after hearing a talk I gave at a local event sponsored by an organisation that sought to increase awareness about diversity.

I suggested psychoanalysis as a useful treatment for the kinds of issues Mr Sullivan was trying to deal with. He decided to start at three times a week, on the couch, and we began to meet on Mondays, Wednesdays, and Fridays. As the material permitted, I continued to explore with Mr Sullivan why three times a week felt better to him, compared to four or five. The Monday session I am describing took place about six months into our work together, after not having met the previous Friday due to a long weekend break.

"I am thinking about stories I have read, about astronauts in space," Mr Sullivan began. "When they're together in close quarters, they often get into fights and have to receive counselling for that." Pause. "Not sure why I thought of that. I've been thinking of this woman, Lizzie, at work, who sends long, overly detailed e-mails about small work-related issues. She's very anxious. She reminds me of women who run the sales offices of apartment buildings. Over the long weekend, I went to a few, because my current lease will expire soon and I've been looking at new places. These women are nice, they say hello, how are you, how can we help you? But they really don't care. Basically, they just want someone to rent their apartments. And Lizzie is like that. The long emails are all about rules, how things should be done."

A pause. He shifted on the couch and seemed to be thinking. "I was having thoughts this weekend that it would probably be better if I saw you more. I missed the Friday session." I noted in my mind that he could not talk about missing *me*, but was aware only of missing "the session". It made sense for him to remain detached in this way, I thought, since he was telling us that people who come too close to each other get into terrible fights. And he obviously didn't feel he could trust me, because maybe all I wanted was for him to rent my vacant hours. At the same time, he was trying to figure out the rules between us. I said nothing and waited.

"But I worry about talking too much if I come more often," he continued. "And you would say, 'So what's wrong with that?'" Silence. "Sometimes, I have images in sessions. Last session, I had an image of you sitting in your chair, relaxed, arms on your sides and then suddenly, a spear pointed under your chin, thrusting your jaw up. I saw myself on a stool by your feet, holding the spear up to your chin. It made me think of movies where somebody is holding a knife to someone's jaw and moving it along the jaw line, up and down." I asked if there was a particular movie he was thinking about. "No, no particular movie; just that it could be dangerous. No skin has been broken yet, nothing's been pierced yet, there's no blood yet."

I felt a sense of shock, of being jarred out of my relaxed analytic listening. "*Yet?*" I asked. "So it could happen, all of this that hasn't happened yet." I wasn't sure where we were heading, but realised that I had cupped my chin in my hand, my fingers spread out over the side of my jaw, as though to protect myself from the dangerous assault Mr Sullivan was contemplating.

A few moments of silence followed. "I have a friend," Mr Sullivan then said, "who knows a lot about religions. Nabil. We were discussing different religions the other day. He's from Egypt originally. I was telling him about my not going to church, how I feel turned off from Catholicism. He started telling me about Islam, and the Prophet of Islam, Mohammad. He said Mohammad had many wives and he took turns spending a night with each one of them in their rooms. The youngest one, the one he loved the most, he married when she was six and the marriage was consummated when she was nine or ten, sometime after she started menstruating."

I said, "Ayesha." He sounded surprised. "Yes, that was her name!" he exclaimed. "So you've heard about her." Pause. "I mean, here I am, I get worried about having sex even with one woman unless I feel really committed to her, and I get really stuck when I think of having sex with more than one woman at any given point in my life—" His voice trailed off.

"And there he was," I said, "the Prophet of Islam, the Prophet of *my* religion, so *my* Prophet. How could he be with a different woman every night? And what about the fact that he married a child, had sex with a nine-year-old?"

He laughed uncertainly, carefully. "Yeah—I feel almost envious. Of the fact that he had a number of women he was sexually involved with. But I also feel, what the fuck? About this child-marriage issue. What was going on? What kind of a crazy custom was that? But this is not easy for me to talk about with you. This has to do with the history of your religion. I mean, it's so *personal*."

"And analysis," I enquired, "should *not* be personal?"

He laughed again, sounding relieved. "Part of me thinks you've probably examined and questioned your religion and chosen aspects of it that make sense to you and those that don't, just as I am trying to do with mine. And I know we're talking about ancient times. Nabil said that some of Mohammad's marriages were to strengthen political alliances, and others to set an example of marrying war widows so that women would not be left unsupported if their husbands died, but it still seems so *wrong!* Out of control, pagan! And I think, no wonder this religion has spawned terrorists." Pause. "I know every religion has strange and contradictory parts of it. Including Catholicism. But as I began to speak about Islam today, and Mohammad, I wasn't sure how things would go. I mean, I saw you drink wine after that talk you gave, and I saw you were sipping water here in your office during the month of Ramadan, so you weren't fasting. So you're not an Orthodox Muslim. But this is about all you must have grown up believing in. And I just wasn't sure how you would react. Could you hear me out without getting defensive?"

"You're *still* not sure," I said. "Can I really be here for you and with you, whatever you might say to me?"

"Yes" A pause. "Nabil also told me that at one point, Mohammad became interested in a woman who was the wife of an adopted son of his. He then said it had been revealed to him [by Allah] that adoption is not allowed in Islam. So an adopted son could never be considered a son at all, and therefore his wife was not off limits. And this woman divorced her husband and married Mohammad."

"So many revelations," I said quietly, referring both to Mohammad's revelations and my patient's, the stories his friend had told him that he was now "revealing" to me. In his mind, I thought, he was upping the ante. How would I respond to his story of Mohammad's marriage to the child Ayesha, and how would I deal with his announcement about Mohammad's interest in his adopted son's wife? Was there a point at which I might not like what he was saying? Would I try to convince him the stories were not true, or feel personally attacked and defensive, as though I had to defend or explain Mohammad's actions?

"Well, this is sort of about where you *live*," he said. "So I'm thinking now, okay, she's talking to me, she seems to be handling it all right, but how is she really feeling?"

"That," I said, "is a very helpful question. How would you really *like* me to feel?"

"You don't seem put out," he said slowly, almost puzzled.

"And *you* don't sound very happy about that," I responded, a clearer awareness of what was happening now dawning on me.

"How can you say that?" he asked angrily. "How do you know that?"

"It might help to think about the two times you laughed earlier," I said. "You were giving us some clues there that haven't been put into words yet."

He was quiet. Then he said, "It was a kind of anxious laughter. First I was afraid, and then I was relieved. I was afraid you would be upset and I was relieved that you weren't."

"I think you were relieved that when you pointed the spear of your words at me, talking about something you thought I might feel hurt by, and angry about, I could listen to it and still sit with you as your analyst. That we could be in close quarters and not get into fights, like the astronauts. That was good news for you," I said. "But it was also bad news. Disappointing news. Because you also *want* me to feel pricked and prodded, shamed, and helpless. Like *you* used to, when your father would attack you at your mother's instigation. So you take with me the role your mother used to take during your childhood. She was simply reporting things to your father that would get you into trouble. As though *she* wasn't angry at you. Just as *you* are *not at all* angry at *me* today."

There was a long silence. I took a deep breath and sat back in my chair, not entirely sure what would happen next. Finally, he spoke.

"Whoa! You really cut to the chase, don't you?" Another silence. Then sadly, reflectively, he said, "It's true. I *am* mad at you. I'm not sure why. But something about the missed session. Your being away. I thought you must be with your daughter, the little girl I saw in the driveway one day. Doing mother–daughter things."

"Ah," I said, "The kind of things your mother would do with your sisters while you were left alone or left to your father's beatings."

He started crying, the first tears in the analysis. We were quiet together. Then he said, "When I masturbate, I imagine a woman going down on me. I feel that's degrading for women. In real life, I wouldn't let a woman do that because I'd be worried she'd find it degrading. Though I know that actually women find it exciting. In my fantasy though, it *is* degrading, and *that's* what excites me. It's sort of like I'm just fucking these women. Just fucking, banging them. It's not about love. Just sex. Like animals. Throwing her down and just fucking her hard. Like they're used needles, throwing them away." I noticed his going from plural to singular to plural again (them, her, them) and kept it as a question for later (wondering whether he was referring to his mother, me, his sisters?)

"You want to demean women, leave them hurt and degraded," I noted.

"Yes," he acknowledged. "I'm thinking about my remarks about Islam, the terrorists, indirectly about you. I think you've been through an analysis, so you must have worked these things out for yourself. I don't need to worry about you. But for some reason I do. I'm worried about hurting you."

"You don't want to hurt me in a way that would make me useless to you," I ventured.

"Yes, not too badly. But at the same time, I *do* want to hurt you with my remarks. I'd like to fuck with your mind. It's like the spear I imagined pointing at your jaw. I feel that's what my words were like."

"What you *hope* they would be like for me," I clarified. "You hope I would feel degraded, demeaned. And the beauty of it is, you would be able to do that, in your mind, simply by telling me the truth, the facts about the religion you know I was born into, whether or not I practice it. *Just the facts.*"

He began to cry again. "That's what my mother used to say when she would complain about me to my father. 'Why are you yelling?' she would say. I'm just telling him the facts."

"And you, so young and without recourse," I reflected. "Such a terrible and helpless position for you to be in. The rage you must have felt, the sense of feeling utterly unloved, unprotected."

After a silence, he asked, "So, are we still on with this idea of my coming more often? Could we plan for that?" I said we certainly could, the next time we met, since we had to stop at that point.

It wasn't until Wednesday, in the relative calm following the stormy Monday session and after we had discussed how to gradually add two more hours to his analytic week, that I realised I had not asked Mr Sullivan what it meant to him that I was the namesake of Ayesha, the prophet Mohammad's child bride. At some point during the session, I asked him about this. His associations led to the idea that maybe her life was planned for her in a way she had no control over, as a child. This reminded him of his own childhood. However, he had been reading about this woman, he said. It seemed that as she grew up, she was very smart, with an inquiring mind, and had a way with words. Mohammad often told people to seek counsel from her. And Mohammad died in her arms, as was his wish.

"He really loved her," Mr Sullivan said. He added that it made him think somebody must have really loved *me*, to name me after this woman—and that made him feel very envious of me, the idea that perhaps I had been loved so well by someone. This opened up a new and useful chapter in the analysis, that of considering his identification with the young female child who became the dearly beloved wife of a powerful man, a prophet, and his sense of me as a female who must have been deeply loved by someone in the way he felt he had not been and in the way he thought his sisters had.

Writing up this material, however, I am struck yet again that even when I thought I understood what Mr Sullivan was doing and feeling, and believed I had managed to function optimally as an analyst, I can now see more points in this session where my analytic functioning was strained. For instance, I wonder now why, in the image he described, he had placed himself on a stool—and why did he choose my jaw, rather than another body part, to point a spear at? Also, why did he appear "surprised" that I had heard of Ayesha? These would have been useful questions to ask. I believe it was his sadism, and my difficulty with it, that constrained me from thinking and speaking more freely. The stories about Mohammad and my religion were one way of expressing his rage about, at best, feeling neglected and abandoned, and, at worst, abused.

Our extreme external differences made it easy to choose this area. But what was actually going on underneath all the "interesting" back-and-forth about religion—and what was most frightening for both of us—was the sadistic wish to hurt and control, and getting pleasure from it.

Mr Gupta

Mr Gupta was a 30-year-old Hindu man of Indian origin living in Bangalore, India, who worked as an information technology expert. I had evaluated him a number of years earlier, when he worked in the U.S., and at that time, given his childhood history and conflicts about his sexual orientation, I had recommended analysis. He decided instead to meet with me only once a week, citing as a reason that he might be going back to India soon. We met once a week for a year, after which he did indeed go back to India.

I heard from him once after his departure. He asked for a referral to an analyst in India, which I gave him. Ten years later, in February 2009, he called again and told me he had seen a couple of people in the interim period but had not found those treatments helpful, and wanted to begin an analysis. Would I be willing to work with him? And if so, how? I was moved by Mr Gupta's capacity and need to hold me, and my initial recommendation, in his mind for ten years, and saddened by his prolonged emotional suffering. I told him that I was now doing some analytic work over the phone and would be happy to speak with him. We could then decide how to proceed.

I was curious as to why Mr Gupta had contacted me at this time, and learned that his anxieties about feeling sexually attracted only to men—anxieties he had spoken about as a young twenty-year-old—were still alive and well. So were his profound narcissistic vulnerabilities when he felt ignored. In response to my question, "Why now?" Mr Gupta said that the day before the Mumbai terrorist attacks of November 2008—in which Muslim terrorist attackers invaded India from Pakistan's seawaters and carried out more than ten coordinated shooting and bombing attacks across Mumbai, India's largest city, that had killed 164 and wounded 300—he had been feeling very angry at his boss, who was giving preferential treatment to a colleague of Mr Gupta's. He was also feeling angry that Arjun, a male colleague he was attracted to, seemed to be vacillating between responding to Mr Gupta and drawing away from him. Then came the Mumbai terrorist attacks.

He was glad he did not live in Mumbai and wondered how any human being could behave in the way the Muslim terrorists had. I asked how he felt about reconnecting with me—an analyst of Pakistani origin—a few months after the attacks, which had been traced back to Muslims from Pakistan. He said he had been thinking about me a lot over the last few months and feeling more and more that he really wanted help; he should have started an analysis ten years ago, as I had suggested. I thought that immense terror had been unleashed in Mr Gupta by the combination of his recent mounting anger about being ignored and excluded and the violence and sadism in the terrorist attacks. Did he feel also that I had excluded/abandoned him ten years ago, when he left America to go back to India?

Mr Gupta's childhood history was still fresh in my mind, with its combination of a professionally successful father who was often out of town and a mother he said he felt loved and helped by, but who would often come out of the shower half dressed and change her clothes in the parental bedroom, where Mr Gupta might be watching TV on the bed. Some of his most painful memories had to do with his father ignoring him on family vacations and instead playing cricket with Mr Gupta's cousins and the sons of family friends, or paying more attention to Mr Gupta's younger brother, his only sibling. He thought this had to do with his father's view of Mr Gupta as unathletic and not as funny as his brother.

We now began a telephone analysis five times a week, with the understanding that Mr Gupta would come to the U.S. once a year so that we could meet in person. The following session took place a little more than a year into the analysis. The session was to be followed by a ten-day break on my part, which Mr Gupta had known about for six months. The session below took place on the Friday before my break.

Mr Gupta began by saying that he had seen a movie, *My Name Is Khan*, the day before. The story was about a couple in New York, a Muslim man and his Hindu wife, whose young son had been beaten to death at a local school shortly after 9/11 because he was Muslim. The wife was enraged and felt that their son had died because her husband was a Muslim. She told him to go and prove to the world that not all Muslims were terrorists. So the hero embarked on a journey, during which he uncovered a Muslim terrorist plot, reported it to the FBI, and, ultimately, met the president.

"He went to such lengths to prove his love for his Hindu wife," I mused, "even exposing other Muslims as terrorists." Mr Gupta said, dismissively, that he found the movie preachy and boring. He then went on to talk about a female colleague who wanted to leave the company they both worked for and go to another one, where she thought she might get more perks. He had talked her out of the idea and she was ultimately grateful, because it would have been a self-destructive career move. After a pause, he added that he had played squash that day, which he hadn't done for a long time. His "marker" (the referee's assistant) was happy to see him. "And there's going to be a small party in my honour at work," he added, "to acknowledge how well I have done with this new project."

"It feels good to be wanted and appreciated," I noted. "That makes you very glad."

He laughed and said that it sure did. I wondered about his laughter at this moment. He said, "You said something I was feeling, but could not say. I felt a little embarrassed that you picked up on it—this feeling of wanting to be wanted. How good it feels to be wanted." A long silence followed. He seemed to be thinking, struggling to say something. "I've been reading about this list of fourteen countries," he finally said, "Cuba and thirteen Muslim countries, whose passengers must be scanned by these new body scanners before they can enter the U.S. I wondered if you are an American citizen. But even if you are, you would have to be scanned, especially if you were travelling back to the U.S. from Pakistan. You must go back to visit your family from time to time."

"Perhaps that's where I'll be when I am not here next week?" I asked.

"I did think that," he acknowledged. "I read that some Muslim women in England refused to go through the body scan." Silence. "But then, if they want to get on a flight, they have to allow themselves to be searched. Then the passenger is at the mercy of the authorities. They can even do body-cavity searches, you know." I heard the indirect, ominous threat he was directing against me, his wish for me to be viciously intruded upon and humiliated, disguised as a "helpful" warning from him that I should be prepared for my body cavities to be searched upon my return from the trip he imagined I was embarking on—the trip that was causing a separation between us. I listened.

"India is not on this list," Mr Gupta continued. "And I've been having many thoughts about what you think about the Indian/Pakistani issue? The enmity. What if your thoughts are different from mine? What would happen to my analysis then? Sometimes, I feel you're a very hot-headed person. Certain things seem to get you all stirred up. I've noticed that sometimes when I talk about someone putting me down and I haven't asserted myself, you start talking to me in a way that makes me think you could get very agitated or angry, and I wonder what you'd be like, if you were very angry." There was a brief pause.

"I'm thinking," he said, "about the Mumbai terrorist attacks last year." I said he had called me, looking for help again, very soon after those attacks. He responded, "Yes, exactly. And I know that the information India finally uncovered was that the terrorists belonged to Lashkar-e-Tayyaba, originally located in Pakistan—that the entire plot was planned in Pakistan. But what if we disagree about where the terrorists came from? What if I insist that they were Muslims trained in Pakistan, and you don't want to see it that way? It's one thing when you get all animated trying to help me assert myself, but what if you get really angry as we speak about these major issues we might think very differently about? I don't want to piss you off. I mean, most of the time, I think this is really cool that I am an Indian Hindu and I have an analyst who is a Muslim and originally from Pakistan, and here we are, working together. That's pretty cool."

"Sometimes it feels pretty cool to you, and at other times, you feel it could be very, very dangerous," I said.

Silence. Then Mr Gupta said, "I've been invited to attend a fundraiser for an Indian NGO [non-governmental organisation]. The President of the NGO is a guy named Bashir Iqbal [a Muslim name]. He hasn't invited me personally. I'm not sure I want to go. I would be someone brought in from the outside, my presence there arranged by our marketing department. But I am not a part of that organisation." A pause. "I snubbed Arjun [the man at work whom Mr Gupta was attracted to, but from whom he was not getting a consistent positive response] today, didn't invite him to join me and a few other colleagues when we were headed out for lunch. He's done that to me at times."

"So much here about inclusion and exclusion," I reflected. "Who's part of the in-crowd, who's invited, who's not, and who gets to be with whom? You feel a sense of great hurt when you feel left out or rejected and you automatically take certain steps to ensure that the tables are turned—that you're the one in control and the other person feels snubbed."

"Oh, I really don't have a serious problem with these things," Mr Gupta retorted. "I just dealt with Arjun and made sure that he felt uncertain and unwelcome—"

"Just as *you* felt around *him*," I interjected quietly. "And yet you don't *really* have a problem with this *at all*."

There was a long silence. I wondered if what I had confronted him with made him feel too exposed. When he spoke, he sounded angry and defensive. "I'm just preventing further pain," he said. "He's the one who invited me to dinner last year when we were in England and then would send me text messages talking about the great times we'd had there. But then he became distant and I feel he's not even sincere with me, nor is he really concerned about me." He was quiet. "Okay, I guess you're right. I just repeated what you had actually said. But what the hell else am I supposed to do when I feel left out?" I remained quiet. "I wish we could continue talking next week. This is hard to deal with, all these bad feelings I have when I feel ignored or pushed aside."

"As when I go away and am not here for you," I said. Silence.

Then Mr Gupta said, "I am wondering how it is for you now in America? Are you being discriminated against? Do people think you might be crazy, like a terrorist? I found myself thinking, the other day, do people even call you to see you for treatment? Or do they feel they don't want to come to you for analysis because you're a Muslim from Pakistan?" I now felt the full onslaught of Mr Gupta's sadistic retaliatory attack—his attempt to regain his narcissistic equilibrium in the storm of feeling belittled by being left. He had tapped into the most primitive anxieties I had felt after 9/11, anxieties connected to my personal history and reawakened by the external events of 9/11 and its aftermath.

I paused, swallowed hard, and asked, "And what might happen to me then?" He responded in a matter-of-fact way, as though he were reading some headlines from the newspaper. "Oh, I think you'd be completely wiped out professionally then. Maybe you wouldn't get any patients—and then I suppose you wouldn't have any money, either."

"And that would serve me right, wouldn't it?" I asked, finding now more stable analytic ground. "For leaving you. It's satisfying for you when you imagine I might be subjected to having my bodily orifices intruded upon and violated, or that I might be wiped out professionally—and you speak about it so calmly."

"I don't feel very calm," he said. "I feel very agitated. Actually, I was thinking just now that maybe that's why you agreed to work with me in analysis—because you wanted to make money, and no one else wanted you as their analyst."

I heard his comment, designed to be hurtful and insulting, but covering over his hurt that I might have agreed to see him for ulterior motives, and his deep disbelief that he could be wanted, or loved, for himself. I said, "Yes, because if that were so, then you'd be my *only* patient, wouldn't you?" I asked. "And very, very special to me. I would really want you. Not like the way you felt with your parents." After a long silence, Mr Gupta spoke.

"All my life," he said, "these difficult, sad feelings with so many people, so many real disappointments and rejections. I do wonder sometimes if I imagine now that people are mistreating me even when they're not, people like you who are actually trying to help me."

A common element in the clinical material

In studying the three cases presented above, as well as two others that I will not detail here, I was struck by a significant common element: the three male patients unconsciously used their awareness of my being "foreign"—and a Muslim—in a particularly cruel and venomous way at a point in the analysis when they were struggling, in the transference, with intense feelings of being forgotten or abandoned. At those times, the differences between us and their knowledge of my being a Muslim was used, in profoundly sadistic ways, to "get even" in an attempt to re-establish a sense of control and mastery—and, beyond that, to establish power and the sense of being one up on the narcissistic seesaw on which they felt precariously balanced. It was only much later in these analyses that my foreignness and my being different could be put to use in the service of my being a forbidden, exotic, exciting woman.

On my part, only after the initial storm had abated could I appreciate that Mr Brodsky experienced me not only as an abandoning mother/nanny/maid or a disappointing or dangerous father, but also as a deeply desired sister/mother with whom he wished to make love—but whom he also wanted to hurt and kill—or that what Mr Sullivan was expressing in his desire to pierce my skin with his spear, linked to the story of Mohammad and Ayesha, was not only his wish to hurt me, but also a profoundly exciting wish and fear about crossing generational boundaries and violating the incest taboo with me. And it was also only later that I could understand, with Mr Gupta, that his sadistic fantasy of my bodily orifices being viciously searched and attacked had to do not only with his rage at feeling excluded from my life and my body, but also his wish to find a way into me and within me.

Discussion

There is both fear of and fascination with differences and strangeness; this is universal, yet individually determined for each of us. These may include the patient's perception of differences in gender, external appearances, ways of thinking, skin colour, racial background, cultural background, and religion. To understand the individual meanings these differences have for the patient, starting from the most superficial and accessible and going toward the deepest underpinnings, is one of the tasks of an analysis. Can such a task be accomplished in the presence of gross and obvious differences between the patient and analyst that preclude a shared understanding of a common racial/cultural/religious/ethnic background? Perspectives on this issue have varied over time.

Oberndorf (1954) did not think it was possible: "Transference in its most positive form," he writes, "is most likely to be easily established and examined (analysed) between patient and hospital and patient and physician if their psychological biases do not differ too widely" (p. 757). The belief seemed to be that people coming from different racial backgrounds would be too distant "psychologically" to be able to establish a transference in the analysis that could facilitate an understanding of the patient's conflicts:

> The fear of the stranger, originating in a young child's feeling of security in the accustomed, and need for protection in the face of the unfamiliar person or place, are [sic] almost instinctive [...] the integration of the mentally disturbed individual can best be achieved if he is treated by one of those who understands his motivations rather than by one considered expert in a particular illness. (Ibid. pp. 757–758)

The thinking here seemed to have been that a patient's motivations could only be understood by someone from a similar cultural background.

Between Oberndorf's 1954 paper and the late 1990s, the psychoanalytic literature included only a small group of papers on the impact of cultural, ethnic, racial, or religious differences between analyst and patient. Yet this has always been an important issue in the U.S., since many early analysts were immigrants. There may be many reasons for this paucity of literature, a discussion of which is not within the scope of this chapter. Its scarcity, however, does not detract from our recognition of its importance. Such differences may have influenced analyses conducted by early immigrant analysts and, later on, as analysts began to write about the experiences of white analysts with black patients, and vice versa. Eventually, other analyst/analysand ethnic combinations attracted attention in the literature as well. This has become even more important today, as the candidate population at psychoanalytic institutes diversifies and more patients from diversified ethnic backgrounds enter psychoanalytic treatment.

In the almost sixty years since Oberndorf presented his paper, the way we think about cross-cultural treatment has evolved. Several analysts have attempted, in detailed, scholarly, and moving papers, to describe their experiences of working in a cross-cultural analytic dyad (Akhtar, 1995, 2006; Goldberg, Myers, & Zeifman, 1974; Holmes, 1992; Leary, 1995, 1997a, 1997b, 2000, 2007). For instance, Schachter and Butts (1968) presented a point of view quite different from Oberndorf's:

> Racial differences between analyst and patient involve issues of unconscious meaning at various levels, analogous to differences in sex between analyst and patient. They must be recognised and utilised, but only rarely do they create an either unanalysable hurdle or a serious obstacle to treatment. (p. 802)

Specific issues requiring close attention come up in analyses that take place across ethnic boundaries. In a 1984 paper, Eva Basch-Kahre, a Swedish analyst, described her work with a black African man living in Sweden. In such contexts, she believes that the analyst's lack of knowledge with regard to the specifics of development, childrearing, values, and conventions of the analysand's background make the "analyst blind to those minimal features which usually alert him that the analysand is approaching conflict territory. I believe that these difficulties cause analysis to proceed at a slower pace, but do not thwart it" (p. 61). I agree, and would extend this to include the fact that particular differences between analyst and patient may cause a kind of "cloudiness" on the analytic horizon, which makes it difficult for the analyst to see things that would be more obvious in other analyses; in such cases, obvious differences between the analytic dyad and the meanings those differences have for patient and analyst may not carry the same weight.

In talking about interracial analysis, Fischer (1971) writes:

> I am suggesting that the black-white difference between the ana-lyst and analysand is a contributing and visible structure upon which the more basic and dynamic infantile wishes are projected. To ignore or overestimate either the manifest structure or the latent projection leads to an incomplete comprehension and working through. (p. 736)

With my patients as well, the obvious difference between us presented a visible structure onto which they could project their feelings of exclusion and devaluation—feelings they had suffered from in their own lives. This projection was made initially through the lens of the obvious differences between us. In this regard, Ticho (1971) writes:

> There is no doubt that cultural differences play an important role in psychoanalytic treatment. However, it is the patient who makes his own choice among the many available stereotypes and endows the analyst with certain positive and negative attributes according to his pathology, individual needs and, concomitantly, with the devel-opment of the transference neurosis. (p. 315)

Given the increasing numbers of analysts from different ethnic back-grounds, it is essential that close attention be paid to the issue of the developing analyst's comfort or discomfort in dealing with factors related to differences of ethnicity, culture, and religion. The ability to handle this material with patients increases as the analyst better under-stands his or her own prejudices and conflicts about ethnicity, religion, and culture; this constitutes important work in one's own personal/ training analysis. Bernard (1953) made important recommendations with regard to the contribution of the training analysis and supervision in terms of cross-cultural issues. She writes:

> We know that the personal and training analysis provides the major safeguard against prejudice, but often the unconscious foundations of prejudice have not been worked with adequately. This may be

due in part to controversies that exist as to the analytic handling
of such material and its relevance to the etiology of neurosis [...]
If, therefore, an analyst has insufficiently analysed his own unconscious material pertaining to his own group membership and
that of others, he and his patient may be insufficiently protected
from the interference of a variety of positive and negative countertransference reactions stimulated by the ethnic, religious and racial
elements that are present in the analytic situation, the patient's
personality, and in the specific content of the patient's material.
The supervisory process in analytic training provides a potentially
valuable second line of defence for supplementing the personal
analysis in regard to these countertransference risks, provided the
supervising analyst is himself sufficiently informed and psychologically qualified in these areas. (pp. 258–259)

In a lovely and useful paper, "Anti-semitism in the clinical setting: Transference and countertransference dimensions", Knafo (1999) describes
a Jewish man whose parents were concentration-camp survivors and
whose most exciting sexual fantasies had to do with "naked women
about to die in Nazi gas chambers, at which point he achieved orgasm"
(p. 38). Knafo, who was then a doctoral candidate, "inwardly recoiled in
horror and fear" (p. 38) and could not work with the patient when she
realised that in telling her these fantasies, he was excited by including
her in the fantasy during the session. In later years, Knafo was able to
see that "anti-Semitism can be a valuable means of engaging the analysis
of transference reactions" (p. 57), and recognised that negative transference reactions, "when embedded in anti-Semitic terminology, tend to be
avoided by therapists and analysts" (p. 58). She writes, "I believe this
results from the therapist's inability to move beyond the perception of
a patient's anti-Semitism as solely a social phenomenon to being able to
treat it as he or she would any other clinical manifestation" (p. 58), and
adds, "The great challenge for psychoanalysts, I believe, lies in the capacity to bridge social and psychic reality in order to discover what is most
therapeutically useful for the patient" (p. 60). I believe that the same
holds true for anti-Muslim sentiments expressed in the analytic setting.

Conclusion

In India and Pakistan, henna (an herbal paste) is mixed with water and
applied to the hands of women for certain festive occasions, including

weddings. The henna, which is green in the powder and paste form, is left on the skin for several hours and is then removed; the dye seeps into the skin and colours it. The colour on the skin of one woman can be quite different from the colour on another: on certain skins, the henna is pale orange, and on others it shows up as bright, flame-coloured orange. It is said that on certain hands, the henna "takes" better than on others. It is postulated that the colour depends on some quality intrinsic to the skin.

So it is, I believe, in psychoanalysis: all patients—and all analysts— are "different" from each other, but in each analysis, the use to which the patient and the analyst put these differences is determined by the patient's needs and conflicts. In some analyses, the differences may not emerge in bright colours; in others, they might present in almost dizzying hues because, for the patient, they serve a critical defensive function. I have presented here vignettes from three analyses in which the ethnic difference between my patients and myself became a vehicle through which their feelings of hurt, rage, and sadism came into the analysis. *This was how the ethnic differences between us were put to use.* I also elaborated on how I could more effectively feel and process my patients' sadistic attacks on me post-9/11, due to my internally increased awareness of *my own* conflicts regarding rage and sadism during that time.

In the next chapter, I will discuss yet another significant sociopolitical event, the discovery and killing of Osama bin Laden on Pakistani soil by specially trained Americans who flew into and out of Pakistan on a single fateful night. I will present analytic material to demonstrate how this event affected analyses I was conducting at the time and what it mobilised in many of my patients.

CHAPTER SEVEN

Osama bin Laden's death and its impact on the analytic process

Introduction

On the night of May 1st, 2011, U.S. Navy SEALs flew helicopters into a fortified compound in a town outside Islamabad, Pakistan, and, shortly after midnight on May 2nd, killed Osama bin Laden. When President Obama announced the news in a special broadcast from the White House, I was shocked to learn where Osama bin Laden had been found: in Abbottabad, where I had spent many years of my childhood and teens with my family, and where my family's home, atop a beautiful hill overlooking the Abbottabad Valley, is still my destination on my twice-yearly trips to Pakistan.

The compound in which bin Laden had been living was about twenty minutes by car from my family home, close to the golf course where my father used to play. My sister and I would often accompany him on his golf outings, so that we could play on the golf course and have lunch with him in the club's restaurant. I felt that a place that had so many happy memories for me had been violated, both because of bin Laden's presence and the SEALs' invasion. Most disturbing were the questions raised in my mind about the possible involvement and complicity of the

Pakistani government/military in arranging shelter for bin Laden in the shadow of the Pakistan military academy (the Pakistani equivalent of West Point).

In the days and weeks following bin Laden's killing in Pakistan, my patients responded in different ways to this news as they attempted to deal with it in their work with me. I will present clinical material from two patients, followed by a discussion of some of the salient aspects of our interactions.

Clinical material

Mr Friedman

May 2nd, 2011

The day Osama bin Laden was killed in Pakistan, Mr Friedman, a successful attorney in his forties, came to his session, lay down on the couch, and began by saying he had just heard about Osama bin Laden's being killed that morning. After a pause he said he didn't like anybody dying. Another pause. I waited. His comment seemed tremendously understated to me, and I wanted to see where he went next. "People are very naïve," he finally said. "They're investing in the stock market like crazy and the stock markets are going up. It's silly for people to assume that if the stock markets are going up now, they will continue to go up because of this news. I'm not sure if I should do anything different. Should I take some new or greater risk with my investments? Do something unusual, because I might make a lot of money that way?"

He continued to speak in this vein. After several minutes, I noted that as he was speaking about all of this, there was a stunning silence in his associations about the fact that bin Laden had been killed in Pakistan, the country he knew was my country of origin. He said yes, he had heard about the fact that bin Laden had been found outside Islamabad, and he remembered that that was where I flew into when I visited Pakistan. At this point he coughed and then winced, as though in pain. I asked about it. He said his haemorrhoid was really bothering him today, and that when he coughed, it hurt. He added, "That really irritated me." I asked what really irritated him. He laughed in a rather forced, falsely pleasant way, and said, "The fact that bin Laden was found in Pakistan really pissed me off. Americans are so concrete. Once we had a shoe bomber, and then forever people's shoes have to be searched. Americans have no global perspective." I felt lost, unable to follow the flow of his associations.

He laughed again, for no reason that I could discern. He said, "Israel is much better about this. They know how to hunt down people in more sophisticated ways." Then suddenly, more angrily, he said, "He was found in fucking Islamabad, for heaven's sake!" Mr Friedman had previously assumed that the Americans hadn't been able to find him because he was in some hard-to-reach mountainous area—"But he was in fucking Islamabad, for crying out loud!" Then, more quietly, he said, "I feel *bad* about feeling this way."

I said I thought that that was the first truly honest-with-himself thing he'd said so far in the session. He laughed again, this time in a somewhat relieved tone, and said, "You know, I almost said to you I really *want* to like you—" His voice trailed off. I asked, "Is it that hard to like me today?" There was a silence. I added, "Perhaps having an analyst who's from Pakistan feels like a real pain in the butt today." He seemed to be thinking, then said, "Another attorney emailed me yesterday and asked if I would take on a Muslim client. I said yes, I would, but would the client want to see *me*? You know, Muslims hate Jews." I was a bit stunned by this statement—so certain, stereotypic, and seemingly without any awareness of what it portended for us. I said, "When you say Muslims hate Jews, it makes me wonder what you feel about the Muslim sitting behind you? And what you imagine I feel about you?" He laughed again. "Oh, you're a warm, kind person, and Osama wasn't."

I felt now that he was frightened of what he was feeling; his laughter was incongruous with the content of his statements. He seemed to be all over the place with his feelings, vacillating between different emotions and points of view. I wondered whether he was aware of it. He said that yes, he thought he was feeling very nervous, but wasn't sure why. I said it sounded distressing, what he was feeling. In an effort to understand what he might be feeling frightened of, I asked, "What do you think about the referring attorney's asking you what he did? And would he ask you the same about a Christian or a Jewish client?" He responded, "No, obviously not. I think he was asking me that specifically because the news had just come out about Osama bin Laden, and he knows I'm Jewish and that my mother's family was killed in the Holocaust." Pause. "People are saying if this had taken place eight or nine years ago it would have more meaning. I mean, it's fine that it happened now, but it's not such a big deal."

I said, "It sounds as though you need to downplay the monumental accomplishment this is for America—the diligence and perseverance involved, by the CIA, in following up on this and tracking down Osama bin Laden." He acknowledged, "Yes, people are rejoicing here in front of the White House, but are the Muslims happy? You know there are billions of Muslims all over the world. If only one per cent are radical, that means there is a very small percentage of terrorists."

I began to see that Mr Friedman was caught between a rock and a hard place; he wasn't sure what I felt about all of this. Part of him was glad bin Laden had been killed, but outraged that he had been hiding in plain view in a Pakistani city. At the same time, he seemed to have a need to sound unreasonable—but to whom? I said, "I hear you struggling in your mind in so many different ways today. Could it be you're wondering where I fit into that percentage?" He replied, "It's not your fault that there are Muslims who are terrorists. You're a moderate." I said, "Who *said* it was my fault?" He replied, sombrely now, "Yes, I get it. *I* said that." I said, "It sounds as though first you feel I'm directly responsible for Osama bin Laden's being in Pakistan, and then you have to convince yourself that I'm actually a good person. But part of you feels it *is* sort of my fault."

He now said vehemently, "Muslims can turn on you in a minute. You never know what Muslims can do. That's what I've grown up hearing and there is a part of me that believes that, but this is ridiculous. It's so irrational for me to have this feeling." I now understood how difficult it was for Mr Friedman to be in touch with violently opposing feelings and beliefs within himself, and I could see how he needed to suppress one or the other at a given moment in order to feel okay about himself and about me. Being in touch with all the conflicting feelings at the same time felt too difficult.

I shared my thoughts, and added, "Sometimes external events allow inner issues to come up more clearly in analysis. This might be your big chance in our work again, since something like this hasn't happened in the world before—and it probably won't happen again, in your lifetime or mine." He turned his head around to look at me, and said "I feel relieved when you say that. I needed to check you meant it. You look like you do. I feel you're understanding that this is scary stuff for me. You sound like you want me to use this to help myself. But I'm worried about sounding like my mother and her cousins, who get all paranoid about people who are not Jews. I feel everything good between us would just break up then."

He fidgeted on the couch. "I've been having thoughts about—does your family have a business there in that posh resort town where he was found, with the Pakistani military academy so close by? Were people training in the Pakistani military and joining Osama's terrorist groups?" This last statement was made just as the session drew to a close, and I was glad to hear that Mr Friedman felt more comfortable after "letting go" with his suspicions about me.

May 3rd, 2011

I was feeling that it had been a very tough two days for me as an analyst, with most of my patients having strong and complicated feelings about Osama bin Laden's being found and killed in Pakistan, my country of origin. Although some patients knew only that I was originally from Pakistan, others knew that the town in which he had been found and killed was where I went on my twice-yearly visits to Pakistan. Very few were able to frankly discuss their feelings with me. For the most part, they felt a need to be tactful, diplomatic, and—when it came to expressing their inner feelings on the matter—wishy-washy. It was only when they felt certain that I could truly hear what they had to say that they were able to voice their feelings of rage about bin Laden's hiding in a country the U.S. had been funding and their distrust of me for being from that country. It had been a two days of tough—and, at times, uncomfortable—analytic work, on both sides of the couch.

On this day, Mr Friedman began the session by saying that he had received a letter from the managing partner at his law firm, saying that they were probably going to dissolve the firm. He would have the option of going with one or two of the partners who intended to continue practicing; a few of the senior partners were retiring. He also had the option of going out on his own. The uncertainty made him feel really scared.

Then he said, "I've been watching the coverage on Osama bin Laden. It's very clear that the Pakistani government and/or the Pakistani military must have known something about his being there in this place, Abbottabad. It's not Islamabad. They're jerks, the Pakistani government and the military. I've been thinking, is that why you left Pakistan, because everyone there is an asshole? How's that, for you to know that these are your people?" I said, "What do you think?" He replied, angrily, "I don't know—how should I?" I noted, "You want to know, how do *I* feel about all this? Those are *my* people, and I live here, work here as an analyst, am paid money by you and other Americans. Are *you* also *my* people?" Mr Friedman said, "If I were you, I'd be very frightened. I mean I know other Pakistani doctors, too, but you seem to have a practice in which there are lots of Jewish patients. There are people who might want to hurt you. I mean, actually want to hurt you, here in America."

I felt a sudden sense of fear at this threat. I said "So even the people here, whom I think are my new people, don't really see me as theirs? My previous people, the people I used to be with, are liars, cheats, money-hungry deceivers who take billions from the U.S. government, then thumb their noses at the U.S.; you think maybe that's why I left them, but here I am now with my *new* people, and they don't *want* me. So perhaps I'll be all alone, without my *old* people and not really wanted or welcomed by my *new* people. Right?" Mr Friedman responded, "Right!," seeming to not understand yet that by outlining what I had just had, I was also trying to describe *his* inner state. I went on, "The only person I could turn to then would be *me*. And I think this is what you also feel as you consider having to quit your current firm that you felt you could depend upon—and now having to consider going to a new place, a new firm, either with one of these partners or on your own. Whatever you do next, would you be welcomed by the new people there, and could you settle down there?"

There was a long silence and then I noticed tears rolling down Mr Friedman's cheeks. I leaned forward in my chair, trying to understand what my words had stirred up in him. "I feel so uncertain about my future," he said. "I feel the two partners who are going out on their own and have offered that I could work for them don't really care about me. I'm not sure they're really interested in having me at their firm. All they care about are the clients I might bring with me." I said, "So they are not really *your* people?" He said, "In a way, no. And yet ironically, they are more my people than you are. They're Jews. One of them, Dick, wished me happy holidays in Hebrew and yet I feel he is not 'my' people." I reflected with him how uncertain he was feeling about his life. I could imagine, I said, that it was not easy for him to be in such a state of uncertainty.

His softer, more vulnerable stance of a few minutes ago now changed back and became guarded and attacking. "Well, yes, that's so," he said, "but that makes us kind of the same. You and your other Muslim friends must be feeling worried right now, with bin Laden discovered in hiding in Pakistan. 'Your' people, as you called them a few minutes ago, have sent you to people who might want to hurt you, here. There are lots of Nazis out there, you know. That's what my mother and her family always say."

I said, "And the only people who want to hurt me are outside the walls of this room, yes? Nobody in here wants to hurt me?" He said, "I knew you'd ask me that. I knew." I said, "If you knew, *really* knew, I would be very glad for you."

Mrs Schrier

Mrs Schrier, who was in her thirties, came for help soon after she had married a charming and successful businessman. When they began having problems in their relationship, she felt that maybe some of her difficulties with him had to do with unresolved feelings about her brilliant but depressed older brother, who had committed suicide by hanging himself when she was in her twenties.

May 2nd, 2011

Mrs Schrier began by talking about financial losses she believed she would undergo in the stock market. She had done something with her stocks, thinking that the market would go up because of bin Laden's death, but instead it went down. She'd already lost $5,000. I thought in my mind that she was talking about a man's death that had caused her to lose money in the stock market, and recalled that her brother had been a financial adviser and had invested people's money.

The patient went on to say that she'd been watching news of bin Laden's death, and wondered whether I knew the place where he had been found. It would be interesting to know, she thought, how I might feel about his death. She had never seen anything like this; people were celebrating in the streets like after the fall of the Berlin Wall. I said, "That was after a separation between the East and the West was removed, the fall of the Berlin Wall." She said, thoughtfully and slowly, "Yes, talking about East and West, that's also you and me. You're from the East. You're in the West now, but obviously I am the one who is really from the West."

I said, "Perhaps you are afraid there would be a loss like the $5,000 you lost—but a loss of a different kind, an emotional kind, if you talk here about this today." She responded, in an embarrassed tone, "In a large percentage of my mind, I believe you are liberal and moderate." I asked, "What percentage?" She said—laughingly, questioningly— "ninety-five per cent?" I said, "If you really believe that, I wonder what would make you feel as anxious as you are?" She said, "I know, I know. I'm sure I don't really feel that. I think that it must be ninety-five per cent." I said, "We might do better to take the five and just add a zero to it—fifty per cent. What do you think? Half and half."

She said, "It makes me feel embarrassed that you understand that. It seems like such a high percentage of doubt to have about someone I've been working so long with. I feel ashamed of myself, but it is true, I really don't feel sure of you. It reminds me how much I really don't know you. I feel like celebrating. I really do. If I were talking with a Jewish analyst right now, I'd speak more freely about celebrating, but I don't want to sound stupid, as if there are things about all of this that I don't understand. I don't want to sound like Donald Trump." I asked, "And what about Donald Trump?" She said, "Well, you know the way he sounds so certain of himself, but he's actually so ignorant. I don't want to sound stupid."

I responded, "The thought of feeling stupid, your fear of sounding stupid, reminds me of your comments about the way you used to feel around your brother—that he was so smart and you felt so stupid, as though you had no intelligence when you were with him. And this loss of $5,000 in two days after the death of Osama bin Laden makes me wonder what prompted you to invest in the way that you did."

After a silence, her thoughts went to her brother, David; to David's death; to how, when David was alive, he was the one who was savvy about the market and investments—but that after he died, he, Mrs Schrier had become very savvy with the market. I said, "All the more reason, then, for us to wonder about the sudden, somewhat impulsive, and perhaps reckless investments that you are talking about, the loss of money, and your worry about losing more money." She said, "I don't know why, but what you say makes me think about Pakistan taking billions of dollars from America and harbouring Osama bin Laden and now pretending to be surprised."

I said, "Secrets. And a terrorist hidden behind high walls and a fortified compound; things that people know and pretend they don't know." She said, with feeling, "Yes, your people." I said, "Right, my people. So who am I and what am I like, really?" There was a long silence and then she said, "I've been wondering how many of your patients are going to leave you now, seeing that you belong to a country that is capable of such deceit and betrayal. How many will drop out of treatment with you?" I felt shock and pain and anxiety; it was as if she'd hit a raw nerve, and I realised how worried I was about this. I steadied myself emotionally and asked quietly, "How many would you like there to be? Is there a number that would satisfy you?" She said vehemently, "All of them, then I'd be the only one here, the only one."

May 3rd, 2011

Mrs Schrier said that she had realised, after we spoke the day before, that Osama bin Laden—the tall dead man—felt like her brother, David. This had come to her in a way it hadn't before we met. She thought that when she saw people dancing in the street, the stock market would go up, and invested $200,000 in a special kind of stock that goes up three times more than the market—but it also goes down more, as much as four or more times more than the market. She had lost $6,000 early on Tuesday and more later in the day. Today, Wednesday, she had finally sold and taken a $30,000 loss. She felt guilty about the idea of making money off a man's death—that's what had happened when her brother died and she found out he had left her everything. How could she not have known that he was so depressed?

I said, "It's such a bad feeling for you, and I think it's getting connected today with the question of how could Pakistan not have known that there was a terrorist there? You inherited half a million dollars after David's death, didn't you?" She said yes. We spoke about the unusual financial risk she had taken, which had been geared toward self-destruction. I said it sounded like "blood money" related to her guilt about her brother David's death.

May 4th, 2011

Mrs Schrier was ten minutes late, and said she had been confused before the session and thought it was Wednesday instead of Thursday; she wasn't sure why. I said, "For some reason, you were wanting this to be Wednesday—something for us to understand." She said she'd been thinking more about this Osama bin Laden/Pakistan issue: maybe it was good that Pakistan "did not know" that Osama bin Laden was there. This would now, hopefully, get Pakistan to look at itself, like Germany did after the Holocaust. Maybe Pakistan would feel ashamed of itself, and take stock of itself in a different way.

"I'm a Jew," she said, "and you're from Pakistan. How many of your patients have left you because of negative feelings about you now that we know you're a Muslim from Pakistan? I know we were talking about that yesterday, and part of me hopes that no one has left you—but really, part of me does wish all of them would leave you. But even if they don't leave you, you would feel awful that they don't see you as the good person and analyst you are, but just as an ethnic type, just a Pakistani." I asked more about this, and she said it had to do with the idea that I would not be seen for who I really was but would be judged only by something external, my ethnicity. I said, "Then I would be like you," referring to her frequent worries about her appearance and her concern that unless she looked a certain way, she would not be acceptable.

She said she thought that the relationship between us was very uncertain, like between Pakistan and America. She didn't believe that the people she thought were there for her would continue in that role if they knew her negative thoughts. As I asked more about these negative thoughts, she hesitantly shared with me that she realised that she wanted me to feel responsible for how Pakistan had sheltered Osama bin Laden—to feel ashamed, just as she felt responsible for her brother's death and just as she felt ashamed of who she was. She also wanted me to feel like she did when she was a child in a school with very few Jewish children, and I would feel like "just a Paki". She recalled how she didn't feel, when she was growing up, that she "fit in", just as she imagined that I didn't feel like I fit in at that point—*and* just as she hoped that I didn't, in fact, feel that way. As we wove our way through this difficult session, another piece of information was added. She shared with me that she had inherited $200,000 from her brother's life insurance— about the same amount she had recently invested in the market, much of which she had lost.

Discussion

Scarfone (2011) proposes that "writing is, for the analyst, an important part of her analytic activity. If a case report [...] is bound to be a 'live wire,' this means that the very act of reporting has to stay actively linked to the living experience of the analysis. It is a continuation of the analysis in another form" (p. 92). He continues:

> I believe that it is a common occurrence for analytic writers to get some of the most significant insights precisely as they are trying to write about their experience. All of a sudden things seem to organise following a new order; new meanings erupt as if out of the blue. But we know it cannot be out of the blue. It is the continuation of the work done during the session and probably prior to it, reflecting the fact that the time structure in the mind is not linear. (Ibid. p. 92)

Scarfone has captured here, in a characteristically beautiful way, an important analytic realisation: that all of us who are analytic writers continue to function not only as writers, *but also as analysts* as we write about our work.

At no point in the writing of this book have I felt this more than when I was going through process notes and preparing to write this chapter. All the notes from the sessions discussed here had initially been written in rough form—either during each session or later that evening—for about a week after bin Laden's death. I wanted to keep track of how the treatments I was conducting then had been affected by this external event. Revisiting these notes almost two years later was a process of discovery and rediscovery. I became aware, as I expect my readers also have, of the stilted, choppy, start-and-stop tempo of the sessions, both in terms of what my patients said and my responses. This is a sign, for me, of high levels of anxiety—both within my patients and myself—and I believe that more than trying to understand the *content* of these sessions, it will be useful to think about the *process* and what lay behind it.

For me, the discovery of Osama bin Laden in my childhood hometown—indeed, almost within view of my family's home in the hills—was surprising and dismaying. I felt a sense of betrayal and outrage at "my" peaceful valley having harboured a terrorist and then been attacked by American helicopters that slipped in quietly at night. Necessary as this had been, it did not feel right for this to be happening in the town that was my original home. Speaking over the phone with my mother after President Obama made his announcement, I learned that all night long, she and others had seen the dull glow of fire from the helicopter that had been damaged while landing. This had made the event seem even more alive in my mind, and more disturbing.

I continued to wonder, as I worked with patients over the next few days, why all of this, shocking as it was, so profoundly disturbing for me. I realised, over time, that the secrecy and duplicity of the Pakistani military and governmental agencies involved—and the stealth of the CIA and the SEALs—reminded me of the fact that my father had been a colonel in the Pakistani army. He had frequently been stationed in Abbottabad, and settled down there after his retirement. Unacknowledged truths and family secrets came to mind. I had spent much of my life trying first to *erect* walls between parts of my mind—so that I wouldn't have to know and deal with certain truths—and then trying to *remove* those walls so that I could allow myself to remember, know, and deal with those unpleasant truths. Now all of this came together in my mind, and it was this understanding that helped me take the first stumbling steps toward being able to help my patients during this time.

Most of my patients seemed caught between, on the one hand, their natural feelings of anger about bin Laden's having been sheltered by Pakistan and, on the other, their fear of—and wish to hurt me with—their anger. It was only when I could address this problem that they could move on to what bin Laden's discovery and killing connected with in their lives. His three-story compound, with its extremely high concrete walls—which were further heightened by the addition of barbed wire—became a symbol of carefully defended and guarded parts of the mind, both mine and my patients'. The various divisions within the compound, the two security gates, and the seven-foot-high privacy wall around the balcony where bin Laden sat or walked, were like the additional compartments the mind maintains to preserve split and dissociated states. With such a possibility in mind, the work of analysis could carry on, and the tense and confused/confusing conversations of the first few days gradually settled into more useful analytic discourse.

Bromberg writes:

> Enactment is a process that takes place in what I think of as a "cocoon built for two," and it certainly is not unique to the analytic relationship. A patient has had plenty of experience with it before ever meeting his analyst, but it is in the analytic relationship that

there is finally a chance to make use of it in a new way. Because it is dissociated, it pulls both patient and analyst into it like a pair of moths drawn to a flame. [...] This leads almost inevitably to repetitive collisions between the patient's subjectivity and that of the analyst, but because the repetitions are nonlinear they hold a powerful therapeutic potential—the potential to generate a process of relational negotiation. (2011, p. 59)

I do believe that a number of enactments, propelled by a number of underlying factors, took place in the analytic sessions I have transcribed in this chapter. I also feel that *for me*—and *for my patients with me*—this was inevitable *at that time*.

I believe that what happened over time, in these analyses, is that as my patients and I collided, each with our own set of anxieties, fantasies, and realities, something began to change in our minds: first the barbed wire, then the concrete walls, and finally the gates, the maze of passages, the privacy fences of the mind—all softened, lowered, and began to crumble, so that old realities about their lives, and mine, could be confronted more easily—and a new reality could be created *between us*. In this regard, Bromberg (2011) writes:

The therapeutic process of increasing a patient's capacity for mentalization invariably entails collisions between the patient's and analyst's subjectivities. The balance between affective safety and seeing ourselves as others see us is a constantly shifting one, and it is the analyst's attunement to these shifts, not the proper application of technique, confrontative or otherwise, that allows increased mentalization to take place. The best work is always done when collisions happen unexpectedly because the process of negotiation that increases mentalization is much more experience-near. (pp. 59–60)

At a time when a significant and significantly disturbing external event touched all our lives, my patients and I struggled to find our footing, lost it, rediscovered it, misunderstood each other, and gradually began to comprehend each other, and ourselves, better. For this, and for much more, I am grateful to the analytic method and to the thinkers and clinicians who continue to expand its usefulness.

NOTES

Chapter Four

1. At this point in the treatment, as Mrs Green and I tried to understand her fantasies of suicide, I felt that her depressive symptoms were severe enough to warrant the use of antidepressant medication. She remained on medication for about ten months. There were multiple direct and indirect thoughts about the meanings of my prescribing this for her.
2. East-West themes and the differences between our cultural and ethnic backgrounds were also stirred up at this time. There was rich exploration of this in our work together—an area of study I have written about elsewhere (Abbasi, 2008, 2012).

Chapter Six

1. 9/11 refers to September 11th, 2001, when members of Al-Qaeda, a Muslim terrorist organisation, hijacked four passenger planes in USA, so that they could be used as weapons of destruction, in coordinated suicide attacks, on that day. Two planes were crashed into twin towers

of the World Trade Center in New York City. A third damaged part of the Pentagon in Washington. The fourth plane, which was also meant to crash into Washington, ended up crashing into a field in Pennsylania. About 3000 people died in these attacks, and widespread damage and destruction occurred.

REFERENCES

Abbasi, A. (1997). When worlds collide in the analytic space: Notes from a "cross-cultural" psychoanalysis. Presented at the winter meeting of the American Psychoanalytic Association, New York.

Abbasi, A. (1998). Speaking the unspeakable. In: A. Helmreich, & P. Marcus (Eds.), *Blacks and Jews on the Couch: Psychoanalytic Reflections on Black-Jewish Conflict* (pp. 133–147). Westport, CT: Praeger, 2008.

Abbasi, A. (2008). "Whose side are you on?": Muslim psychoanalysts treating non-Muslim patients. In: S. Akhtar (Ed.), *The Crescent and the Couch: Cross-Currents Between Islam and Psychoanalysis* (pp. 335–350). New York: Jason Aronson, 2008.

Abbasi, A. (2011). "Where do the ova go?" An analytic exploration of fantasies regarding infertility. *Psychoanalytic Inquiry, 31*: 366–379.

Abbasi, A. (2012). "A very dangerous conversation": The patient's internal conflicts elaborated through the use of ethnic and religious differences between analyst and patient. *International Journal of Psychoanalysis, 93*: 515–534.

Abend, S. M. (1982). Serious illness in the analyst: Countertransference considerations. *Journal of the American Psychoanalytic Association, 30*: 365–379.

Akhtar, S. (1995). A third individuation: Immigration, identity, and the psychoanalytic process. *Journal of the American Psychoanalytic Association, 43*: 1051–1084.

Akhtar, S. (2006). Technical challenges faced by the immigrant psychoanalyst. *Psychoanalytic Quarterly, 75*: 21–43.

Akhtar, S. (2009a). *The Damaged Core: Origins, Dynamics, Manifestations, and Treatment*. New York: Jason Aronson.

Akhtar, S. (2009b). *Comprehensive Dictionary of Psychoanalysis*. London: Karnac.

Akhtar, S. (Ed.) (2011). *The Electrified Mind: Development, Psychopathology, and Treatment in the Era of Cell Phones and the Internet*. New York: Jason Aronson.

Akhtar, S. (2012). *The Mother and her Child: Clinical Aspects of Attachment, Separation, and Loss*. New York: Jason Aronson.

Allison, G., & Doria-Medina, R. (1999). New reproductive techniques. *International Journal of Psycho-Analysis, 80*: 163–166.

Ambrosiano, L. (2005). The analyst: His professional novel. *International Journal of Psycho-Analysis, 86*: 1611–1626.

Anisfeld, L. (1993). On the therapist's disability: Opportunities for resolution of obstructed mourning in the transference. *Psychoanalytic Review, 80*: 457–473.

Appelbaum, A., & Diamond, D. (1993). Prologue. *Psychoanalytic Inquiry, 13*: 145–152.

Armstrong, P. F. (2000). *Opening Gambits: The First Session of Psychotherapy*. Northvale, NJ: Jason Aronson.

Basch-Kahre, E. (1984). On difficulties arising in transference and countertransference when analyst and analysand have different socio-cultural backgrounds. *International Review of Psycho-Analysis, 11*: 61–67.

Beres, D. (1973). Non-verbal communication. *Psychoanalytic Quarterly, 42*: 629–637.

Bergmann, M. S. (1997). Passions in the therapeutic relationship: A historical perspective. *Canadian Journal of Psychoanalysis, 5*: 73–94.

Berman, L. (1950). Psychoanalysis and group psychotherapy. *Psychoanalytic Review, 37*: 156–163.

Bernard, V. W. (1953). Psychoanalysis and members of minority groups. *Journal of the American Psychoanalytic Association, 1*: 256–267.

Billow, R. M. (2000). Self-disclosure and psychoanalytic meaning: A psychoanalytic fable. *Psychoanalytic Review, 87*: 61–79.

Bird, B. (1957). A specific peculiarity of acting out. *Journal of the American Psychoanalytic Association, 5*: 630–647.

Blum, H. P. (1994). The confusion of tongues and psychic trauma. *International Journal of Psycho-Analysis, 75*: 871–882.

Boesky, D. (1982). Acting out: A reconsideration of the concept. *International Journal of Psycho-Analysis, 63*: 39–55.

Bromberg, P. (2011). *The Shadow of the Tsunami and the Growth of the Relational Mind*. New York: Routledge.

Bromberg, P. M. (2003). One need not be a house to be haunted: On enactment, dissociation, and the dread of "not-me"—A case study. *Psychoanalytic Dialogues, 13*: 689–709.

Buechler, S. (2009). Love will do the thing that's right: Commentary on paper by Stuart A. Pizer, Ph.D., A.B.P.P. *Psychoanalytic Dialogues, 19*: 63–68.

Busch, F. (1989). The compulsion to repeat in action: A developmental perspective. *International Journal of Psycho-Analysis, 70*: 535–544.

Busch, F. (2009). 'Can you push a camel through the eye of a needle?': Reflections on how the unconscious speaks to us and its clinical implications. *International Journal of Psychoanalysis, 90*: 53–68.

Caccia, O. (1999). Unconscious phantasy as an obstacle and as a stimulus to knowledge. *Journal of Child Psychotherapy, 25*: 429–446.

Carr, N. (2010). *The Shallows: What the Internet is doing to our Brains*. New York: W. W. Norton & Company.

Carroll, E. J. (1954). Acting out and ego development. *Psychoanalytic Quarterly, 23*: 521–528.

Chasseguet-Smirgel, J. (1990). On acting out. *International Journal of Psycho-Analysis, 71*: 77–86.

Chused, J. F. (1991). The evocative power of enactments. *Journal of the American Psychoanalytic Association, 39*: 615–639.

Crastnopol, M. (1997). Incognito or not? The patient's subjective experience of the analyst's private life. *Psychoanalytic Dialogues, 7*: 257–280.

Dewald, P. A. (1982). Serious illness in the analyst: Transference, countertransference, and reality responses. *Journal of the American Psychoanalytic Association, 30*: 347–363.

Eissler, K. (1977). On the possible effects of aging on the practice of psychoanalysis. *Psychoanalytic Quarterly, 46*: 182–183.

Eissler, K. R. (1958). Remarks on some variations in psycho-analytical technique. *International Journal of Psycho-Analysis, 39*: 222–229.

Ekstein, R., & Friedman, S. W. (1957). The function of acting out, play action and play acting in the psychotherapeutic process. *Journal of the American Psychoanalytic Association, 5*: 581–629.

Fabricius, J., & Green, V. (1995). Termination in child analysis: A child-led process? *Psychoanalytic Study of the Child, 50*: 205–225.

Fajardo, B. (2001). Life-threatening illness in the analyst. *Journal of the American Psychoanalytic Association, 49*: 569–586.

Fenichel, O. (1954). Neurotic acting out. In: H. Fenichel (Ed.), *The Collected Papers of Otto Fenichel: Second Series* (pp. 296–304). New York: Norton.

Ferro, A., & Basile, R. (2006). Unity of analysis: Similarities and differences in the analysis of children and grown-ups. *Psychoanalytic Quarterly, 75*: 477–500.

Fischer, N. (1971). An interracial analysis: Transference and countertransference significance. *Journal of the American Psychoanalytic Association, 19*: 736–745.

Freud, A. (1968). Acting out. *International Journal of Psycho-Analysis, 49*: 165–170.

Freud, S. (1905). Fragment of an analysis of a case of hysteria. *S. E., 7*: 1–122. London: Hogarth.

Freud, S. (1917). Introductory lectures on psycho-analysis. *S. E., 16*: 241–463. London: Hogarth.

Gabbard, G. O. (1982). The exit line: Heightened transference-countertransference manifestations at the end of the hour. *Journal of the American Psychoanalytic Association, 30*: 579–598.

Gaddini, E. (1982). Acting out in the psychoanalytic session. *International Journal of Psycho-Analysis, 63*: 57–64.

Gervais, L. (1994). Serious illness in the analyst: A time for analysis and a time for self analysis. *Canadian Journal of Psychoanalysis, 2*: 191–202.

Goldberg, E. L., Myers, W. A., & Zeifman, I. (1974). Some observations on three interracial analyses. *International Journal of Psycho-Analysis, 55*: 495–500.

Goldstein, W. N. (1998). *A Primer for Beginning Psychotherapy*. Washington, D.C.: Taylor & Francis.

Greenacre, P. (1950). General problems of acting out. *Psychoanalytic Quarterly, 19*: 455–467.

Gurtman, J. H. (1990). The impact of the psychoanalyst's serious illness on psychoanalytic work. *Journal of the American Psychoanalytic Association, 18*: 613–625.

Halpert, E. (1982). When the analyst is chronically ill or dying. *Psychoanalytic Quarterly, 51*: 372–389.

Hollender, N. H., & Ford, C. V. (2000). *Dynamic Psychotherapy: An Introductory Approach*. Northvale, NJ: Jason Aaronson.

Holmes, D. E. (1992). Race and transference in psychoanalysis and psychotherapy. *International Journal of Psycho-Analysis, 73*: 1–11.

Horowitz, M. H. (1996). Some notes on transference and memory: A tribute to Leo Stone. *Journal of Clinical Analysis, 5*: 197–211.

Jacobs, T. J. (1991). *The Use of the Self: Countertransference and Communication in the Analytic Situation*. Madison, CT: International Universities Press.

Kahn, N. E. (2003). Self-disclosure of serious illness: The impact of boundary disruptions for patient and analyst. *Contemporary Psychoanalysis, 39*: 51–74.

Kantrowitz, J. L. (2009). Internet interaction: The effects on patients' lives and analytic process. *Journal of the American Psychoanalytic Association, 57*: 979–988.

Kanzer, M. (1957). Acting out, sublimation and reality testing. *Journal of the American Psychoanalytic Association, 5*: 663–684.

Kestenberg, J. S. (1968). Acting out in the analysis of children and adults. *International Journal of Psycho-Analysis, 49*: 341–344.

Kieffer, C. C. (2008). On siblings: Mutual regulation and mutual recognition. *Annals of Psychoanalysis, 36*: 161–173.

Kieffer, C. C. (2011). The waiting room as boundary and bridge between self-states and unformulated experience. *Journal of the American Psychoanalytic Association, 59*: 335–349.

Kjellqvist, E. (1995). The regeneration of a soul's history. *Scandinavian Psychoanalytic Review, 18*: 160–175.

Knafo, D. (1999). Anti-Semitism in the clinical setting: Transference and countertransference dimensions. *Journal of the American Psychoanalytic Association, 47*: 35–63.

Kucera, O. (1968). On being acted on. *International Journal of Psycho-Analysis, 49*: 495–497.

LaFarge, L. (2000). Interpretation and containment. *International Journal of Psycho-Analysis, 81*: 67–84.

Lasky, R. (1990). Catastrophic illness in the analyst and the analyst's emotional reactions to it. *International Journal of Psycho-Analysis, 71*: 455–473.

Leary, K. (1995). Interpreting in the dark: Race and ethnicity in psychoanalytic psychotherapy. *Psychoanalytic Psychology, 12*: 127–140.

Leary, K. (1997a). Race in psychoanalytic space. *Gender and Psychoanalysis, 2*: 157–172.

Leary, K. (1997b). Race, self-disclosure, and "forbidden talk": Race and ethnicity in contemporary clinical practice. *Psychoanalytic Quarterly, 66*: 163–189.

Leary, K. (2000). Racial enactments in dynamic treatment. *Psychoanalytic Dialogues, 10*: 639–653.

Leary, K. (2007). Racial insult and repair. *Psychoanalytic Dialogues, 17*: 539–549.

Levine, H. B., & Brown, L. J. (Eds.) (2013) *Growth and Turbulence in the Container/Contained: Bion's Continuing Legacy*. London: Routledge.

Levine, H. B., Reed, G. S., & Scarfone, D. (2013). *Unrepresented States and the Construction of Meaning: Clinical and Theoretical Contributions*. London: Karnac.

Linna, L. (2002). When the analyst falls ill: Implications for the treatment relationship. *Scandinavian Psychoanalytic Review, 25*: 27–35.

McDevitt, J. B. (1995). A childhood gender identity disorder: Analysis, preoedipal determinants, and therapy in adolescence. *Psychoanalytic Study of the Child, 50*: 79–105.

Oberndorf, C. P. (1953–1954). Selectivity and option for psychiatry. *American Journal of Psychiatry, 110*: 754–758.

Perelberg, R. J., & Levinson, N. A. (2003). Panel on "Acting out and/or enactment." *International Journal of Psycho-Analysis, 84*: 151–155.

Phillips, S. H. (1998). A new analytic dyad: Homosexual analyst, heterosexual patient. *Journal of the American Psychoanalytic Association, 46*: 1195–1219.

Pizer, S. A. (2009). Inside out: The state of the analyst and the state of the patient. *Psychoanalytic Dialogue, 19*: 49–62.

Rosner, S. (1986). The seriously ill or dying analyst and the limits of neutrality. *Psychoanalytic Psychology, 3*: 357–371.

Roughton, R. E. (1993). Useful aspects of acting out: Repetition, enactment, and actualisation. *Journal of the American Psychoanalytic Association, 41*: 443–472.

Scarfone, D. (2011). Live wires: When is the analyst at work? *International Journal of Psycho-Analysis, 92*: 755–759.

Scarfone, D. (2012). Where the streets have no name. Presented at a panel on "Non-verbal elements in analysis." National meeting of the American Psychoanalytic Association.

Schachter, J. S., & Butts, H. F. (1968). Transference and countertransference in interracial analyses. *Journal of the American Psychoanalytic Association, 16*: 792–808.

Schwartz, H. J., & Silver, A. -L. S. (Eds.) (1990). *Illness in the Analyst: Implications for the Treatment Relationship*. Madison, CT: International Universities Press.

Segel, N. P. (1969). Repetition compulsion, acting out, and identification with the doer. *Journal of the American Psychoanalytic Association, 17*: 474–488.

Stein, M. H. (1973). Acting out as a character trait: Its relation to the transference. *Psychoanalytic Study of the Child, 28*: 347–364.

Strean, H. S. (1981). Extra-analytic contacts: Theoretical and clinical considerations. *Psychoanalytic Quarterly, 50*: 238–259.

Strean, H. S. (2002). A therapist's life-threatening disease: Its impact on countertransference reactions and treatment techniques. *Psychoanalytic Inquiry, 22*: 559–579.

Sugarman, A., Nemiroff, R. A., & Greenson, D. P. (1992). *The Technique and Practice of Psychoanalysis*. Madison, CT: International Universities Press.

Ticho, G. R. (1971). Cultural aspects of transference and countertransference. *Bulletin of the Menninger Clinic, 35(5)*: 313–334.

Torrigiani, M. G., & Marzi, A. (2005). When the analyst is physically ill: Vicissitudes in the analytical relationship. *International Journal of Psycho-Analysis, 86*: 1373–1389.

Turkle, S. (2011). *Alone Together: Why We Expect More from Technology and Less from Each Other*. New York: Basic Books.

Usher, S. (2005). [Review of the book: *Illness in the Analyst: Implications for the Treatment Relationship* edited by H. J. Schwartz & A. -L. Silver]. *Canadian Journal of Psychoanalysis, 13*: 363–368.

Waelder, R. (2007). The principle of multiple function: Observations on over-determination. *Psychoanalytic Quarterly, 76*: 75–92.

Weinberg, H. (1988). Illness and the working analyst. *Contemporary Psychoanalysis, 24*: 452–461.

Weiss, S. S. (1975). The effect on the transference of "special events" occurring during psychoanalysis. *International Journal of Psycho-Analysis, 56*: 69–75.

Wilson, J., & Ryz, P. (1999). Endings as gain: The capacity to end and its role in creating space for growth. *Journal of Child Psychotherapy, 25*: 379–403.

Winnicott, D. W. (1953). Transitional objects and transitional phenomena: A study of the first not-me possession. *International Journal of Psycho-Analysis, 34*: 89–97.

INDEX

163